SATISFACTION

SATISFACTION

TOWARDS A BIOLOGY OF MIND AND LANGUAGE

WILLIAM REYNOLDS

Jenny and Jeremy

very best wishes

William

BURLESTONE PRESS
DARTMOUTH

Published in 2009

Burlestone Press
PO Box 69
Dartmouth
TQ6 6AB
United Kingdom

Copyright © W S G Reynolds 2009

The moral right of the author has been asserted

All rights reserved. No part of this publication may be reproduced, stored in a retrieval system or transmitted, in any form or by any means, without the prior permission of the publisher.

A CIP catalogue record for this book is available from the British Library

Library of Congress Cataloguing in Publication Data: applied for

Design and typesetting (Sabon 10.5/13.5) by Sue Snell
Printed and bound in Great Britain by TJ International, Padstow
Printed on acid-free paper

ISBN: 978 0 9562040 0 4

www.burlestone.com

CONTENTS

Preface	vii
Glossary	ix

1 Why life is exceptional — 1

Cognitivism and AI	2
Ontology and epistemology	5
The mind–body relation	8
Neuronal activity	11
Phenomenal consciousness	12
Sensorimotor feedback	16
The inherence of meaning	20
The S-axis introduced	23
The brain as satisfaciend	27
Phenotypic plasticity	31
Direct and indirect perception	37
Perception and proprioception	44
Inclusive phenomenality	48
Perception as function	50

2 Extending the phenotype — 54

Ephemerality and directionality	57
Semantic meaning	61
Sense and reference	64
Linguistic intension	70
Facts and propositions	74
The propositional attitude	82
Modality and apriority	86
Pragmatics	90
Speech acts	94
A note on art	98
Non-human naming	102

3   They thought they were machines   104

   Intention   105
   Action, intension and motor behaviour   108
   Reasons for action   115
   Directives and intention   118
   Institutions, games and rules   124
   The status of the extended S-axis   129
   Science and epistemology   131
   Causation and science   137
   Counterfactual dependence   141
   Downward metaphysical necessity   144
   Freedom of action   149
   Biological deconstraint   152

Recommended reading   156
References & Bibliography   158
Index   161

PREFACE

The genesis of this book may be of interest. I read Literae Humaniores, roughly translated as Classics, at Brasenose College, Oxford in the 1970s (and have had no subsequent academic affiliation). This involved being introduced to a subject (philosophy) that would become a permanent source of pleasure and stimulation. Years later, having also developed an interest in evolutionary biology, I wanted to communicate some of that pleasure in a short introductory book. When I started writing, I found that the process helped me to think more productively; to my surprise an original theory with explanatory power gradually took shape. As I revised the text, it became primarily a vehicle for the theory. Not wishing to lose sight of my original intention, I tried to keep technical language to a minimum and avoid unnecessarily complicated argument in a way that reflected the comparative simplicity of the theory. Some readers interested in the idea or in finding out more about philosophy may nevertheless find the book daunting. I have been told that it is not for a non-specialist readership but I remain convinced that, if sufficiently motivated, an intellectually curious reader will be able to cope.

The first chapter contains far more biology than the other two, specifically basic neurology and evolutionary/developmental biology: if it interests you less than philosophy, avoid getting bogged down at that stage. I should indicate briefly why it is essential to the plot. Most if not all philosophy of mind assumes that the internal workings of organisms are subject to the same causal laws that govern, or manifest themselves in the behaviour of, inorganic matter. This effectively makes biology irrelevant to the philosophy of mind. I believe and try to show that on the contrary something distinctive occurs inside organisms, with significant implications for philosophy, including its general treatment of causation. Biology in my view holds the key to progress in philosophy. This is not a way of saying that philosophy can be reduced to biology or of calling its independence into question. Neither do I espouse a version of evolutionary psychology. I hope these matters are clarified in the following pages.

I would like to thank my editor, Jonathan Price. I would also mention Guillermo Osorno, who in a sense got me to write. I doubt whether I am the only one.

The Glossary contains some terms which occur in places other than where they are defined, or are not defined in the text. Other key terms will be found in the Index. A date in parentheses signifies a reference to a publication listed under the author in the References & Bibliography section.

The cover image instantiates various issues surrounding the resolution of inputs to the visual system.

WSGR
April 2009

GLOSSARY

a priori/a posteriori
:   A *priori* knowledge is independent of experience; *a priori* judgments cannot be falsified by experience. *A posteriori* knowledge is dependent on experience or empirical evidence.

afferent/efferent
:   Of the direction taken by neuronal impulses travelling between the brain and the periphery of the body. Afferent pathways carry impulses from the sense organs to the brain, while efferent pathways control motor behaviour.

behaviourism
:   The doctrine that descriptions of mental properties are to be understood as descriptions of dispositions to behaviour.

binding
:   Integration by the brain of various sensory inputs, especially visual inputs, in respect of the various properties of a single object.

cognition
:   The mental process of knowing or becoming aware, whether through perception, memory, reasoning or intuition.

cognitivism
:   The doctrine that cognition is essentially an information-processing activity, which by implication could be realized computationally.

contingent
:   True only under certain conditions; not necessarily or universally true (of sentences or statements).

correlation
:   A causal, complementary or parallel relationship between two variables, such that the occurrence of one is accompanied by the occurrence of the other, or that alterations to their states co-vary.

dualism
:   The doctrine that the world consists of, or is only explicable in terms of, two fundamental entities, normally mind and matter.

efferent *see* afferent

emergence
:   The creation of new phenomena, requiring new laws and principles, at the higher levels of organization of a complex system.

epistemology
   The branch of philosophy concerned with the nature of knowledge, its presuppositions, foundations, extent and validity. This book throughout contrasts epistemology with ontology, that is, the world as cognitively realized and the world as it is in itself, independently of minds.

extension
   An object's extension is the property by which it occupies space. The extension of a name is the part of the world to which it refers. In this book the adjective 'extensional' (in contrast with 'intensional') denotes the use of a verb to describe behaviour without reference to the attitude of the agent.

externalism
   The doctrine that what is thought or experienced is dependent on, and may be causally individuated by, aspects of the world external to the mind of the subject.

gene expression
   The process by which heritable information from a gene, such as the DNA sequence, is used in the synthesis of a functional gene product, such as protein or RNA.

genotype
   The genetic makeup, as distinguished from the physical appearance, of an organism or a group of organisms.

idealism/realism
   Idealism denotes any doctrine according to which reality is fundamentally mental in nature. An idealist might hold that we have no rational grounds for believing in the reality of anything but ideas and their relations. Realism is opposed to idealism but may take many forms.

incorporand *see* **satisfaciend**

intension
   Conventionally, any property or quality connoted by a word or phrase, as distinct from the extension of a word or phrase. In this book intension denotes the activity of meaning by a subject, whether in language use or motor behaviour.

intentionality
   The property of being about or directed toward a subject, as inherent in conscious states, beliefs or creations of the mind.

internalism
   The doctrine that mental states are individuated by conditions internal to the subject of those mental states. The internalist accepts that external conditions influence mental states, but rejects any principled correlation between them.

GLOSSARY

metaphysics
　The branch of philosophy that examines questions about reality that lie beyond or behind those capable of being addressed by the methods of science. These include the ultimate nature of reality, the relation of mind and matter, the nature of causation and truth, and the presuppositions of scientific method.

modality
　The classification of sentences or propositions according to the way in which they are true or false, that is, whether they assert or deny the possibility, impossibility, contingency or necessity of their content.

motor behaviour
　Any bodily movement with its origin in the brain.

naturalize
　Explain with reference to nature, as interpreted by empirical science.

normative
　Couched in terms expressive of requirements or standards.

ontology
　The branch of metaphysics that deals with the nature of being. In this book a feature of the word is ontological or real if it exists independently of minds.

parse
　Make sense of by analyzing. In this book, parsing denotes the activity of animals in organizing sensory inputs to adaptive states of awareness which may prompt beneficial behaviour.

percept
　An external object as it presents itself in perception, to be considered apart from how it may be in itself.

phenomenal/reflective
　Phenomenal consciousness describes the qualitative nature of subjective experience, derived through any of the senses. It is distinguished from reflective consciousness, in which we think, believe and intend.

phenotype
　The observable physical characteristics of an organism, as determined by both genetic makeup and environmental influences. The phenotypic extension is an functional adjunct deployed by the organism. Phenotypic plasticity denotes the various ways in which an organism optimizes its phenotype through the mechanisms of gene expression, normally in response to environmental changes. In this book plasticity is attributed in particular to adaptational brain function.

physicalism/materialism
: Materialism is the doctrine that physical matter is the only reality and that everything, including thought, feeling, mind and will, can be explained in terms of matter and its behaviour. Physicalism extends the principle to other physical phenomena such as forces and wave/particle relationships.

proprioception
: An organism's sense of the position and movement of its limbs and its sense of muscular tension. Proprioception may influence motor behaviour without reaching consciousness.

realism *see* **idealism**

reductionism
: The doctrine that the facts or entities apparently needed to make true the statements of some area of discourse are dispensable in favour of some other facts or entities.

referent
: A person or thing to which a linguistic expression refers.

referentialism
: The doctrine that the referent of a linguistic expression is a component of that expression's meaning.

representationalism
: The doctrine that the mind works on representations of the things and features of things that we perceive or think about, rather than on the things themselves.

satisfaciend/incorporand
: Terms introduced in this book to denote, respectively, a biological type that stands in an axial relation to a functional condition of satisfaction, and a contingent factor expected by a satisfaciend in order to realize its condition of satisfaction. The term 'S-axis' denotes the axial relation.

semantic
: Of or relating to meaning, especially meaning in language.

sensorimotor
: Of, relating to, or involving both sensory and motor activity.

sentience
: The capacity to feel or perceive subjectively, used in particular in discussions of whether other animals possess sentience or phenomenal consciousness.

teleology
: The study of design or purpose in natural phenomena. The use of design or purpose as a means of explaining phenomena. In this book teleology is adopted as one way of characterizing biological function.

CHAPTER 1

WHY LIFE IS EXCEPTIONAL

Western science originated in speculation about the nature of matter and the cosmos in the Greek-speaking communities of the eastern Aegean around 600 BC. The figures at the centre of this phenomenon could describe themselves as philosophers or 'lovers of wisdom' because in a superstitious culture they sought a rational understanding of the physical universe. They competed for pupils and influence in a market of ideas as free as cultural inhibitions would allow; a trade in theory complemented the burgeoning commerce of the seaboard city-states. Amid this ferment Democritus of Abdera (b. 460) was notable for proposing that matter consisted of atoms, which moved randomly in empty space and could be conjoined. As these societies began to experiment with novel forms of government and the intellectual centre of gravity shifted to Athens, thinkers turned their attention to ethics and politics. The decisive influence was that of Socrates (d. 399), who seems to have shown little interest in physics and cosmology, preferring to apply the principles of rational enquiry to human life. In the fourth century Aristotle pursued the Socratic agenda as mediated by Plato in a more systematic way, while finding time to invent biology and create a system of logic that was superseded only in the nineteenth century. When his surviving works eventually penetrated Europe in the thirteenth century, being seized upon most notably by Aquinas, they contributed to an intellectual revolution. The world in its complexity, including human life and society, was seen to subsist on its own terms and to merit study without unargued assumptions. The Renaissance was underway.

The subsequent rise of science, symbolized by the Copernican revision of cosmology, can be attributed partly to the unflinchingly analytical, emancipatory spirit inherited from Greek enquiry. Compare Chinese science, which, although impressive in its way, was always licensed and patronized by a unitary authority. In the West it was religion that offered resistance (temporal powers had a competitive military interest in technological advance), in a pattern sustained until the twentieth century in Europe and to the present day in America. The cultural turning-point occurred in the late seventeenth and early eighteenth century. When the universe was found to obey laws brokered by science, philosophy was inevitably cast in the role of onlooker to the main business. Although in principle it could claim to oversee the methodology of science and define its boundaries, in fact science developed a regulatory logic of its own, vindicated by its spectacular success. Philosophy has since been drawn into its orbit, to the point where its integrity is now arguably under threat. Even morals and ethics are considered by many to have been subsumed by 'evolutionary psychology'. Outstanding problems in philosophy are widely believed to await scientific resolution.

Cognitivism and AI

The principal unsolved philosophical problem is agreed to be the nature of the mind and its relation to the brain. It was not inevitable that this should also become a problem for science: psychology could have concerned itself with the mind and neurobiology independently with the brain. Matters were transformed by advances in computer science during the Second World War and in particular by the Turing machine, which demonstrated that a computer could be programmed with instructions that would govern its future responses indefinitely. Information seemed to offer the key to understanding the mind because it was at once communicable, computable and capable of driving physical processes. The mind could therefore be investigated as a physical computational mechanism, receiving and encoding sensory inputs, processing them against stored resources and producing outputs in the form of motor and linguistic behaviour. This model became the basis of research into artificial intelligence (AI).

AI has two objectives: firstly to provide solutions, by any computational means available, to what for us are cognitive problems and secondly to replicate our cognitive processes computationally. *Cognition* is an inclusive term for the mind's coming to know, whether through perception, memory, inference or deduction. In the early, optimistic days of AI, there was an expectation that its two aspects would rapidly converge and that the experimental programme would help to uncover the workings of the brain. This virtuous state of affairs was never realized. The manner of its funding has meant that AI research now consists of discrete projects with achievable goals, such as reading handwriting or recognizing faces. To take a well-known example, in 1997 a computer for the first time beat a reigning world chess champion. It was inevitable that this would happen sooner or later with the harnessing of sufficient computing power. It was also clear that grand masters develop strategies in a different way. But neuroscience was unable to produce a theory on which a more realistic model of the brain could be based.

When Marvin Minsky, who co-founded the AI Laboratory at the Massachusetts Institute of Technology in 1959, described AI in 2003 as having been 'brain-dead since the 1970s', he was lamenting its mysterious failure to advance like a genuinely experimental science. He believes the breakthrough may come when machines are able to engage in 'common sense' reasoning. He endorses Douglas Lenat's Cyc project, which since 1984 has been compiling a database of factual information such as 'People live in houses' and 'When it rains, you get wet.' The aim is to record at least 100 million such items, estimated to be the number held by the average person. The task will then be to understand and model the processes by which humans select the handful of facts most relevant to a given situation. Somehow an autonomous intelligence may then take off and start to provide itself with knowledge. Lenat hinted at the reason why so many factual items are needed when he revealed that Cyc had had to be disabused of the notion that everyone born before 1900 was famous – a pardonable inference given that the only people born before 1900 about whom it had been briefed were famous.

In a report commissioned by the British government, James Lighthill (1973) foresaw many of the shortcomings of AI and recommended that research be discontinued except in three universities. He pointed in particular to the problem of *combinatorial explosion*, or of controlling the exponential increase in computational demand when a model integrates several functions. AI has since been a term normally avoided in British institutions. Lighthill also coined the expression 'cognitive science', intending it to cover relevant activity across a range of disciplines, including neuroscience, philosophy, psychology and linguistics. The unifying factor, and the hallmark of *cognitivism*, is the assumption that cognition is a form of information processing, which by implication could be realized computationally.

Critics of cognitivism look for features of the human mind that 'intelligent' machines both lack and seem unlikely in principle to acquire. Foremost among these is consciousness. There are conscious states and there are conscious beings, capable of entertaining conscious states. A person may be said to be conscious in the clinical sense of not being asleep or otherwise unconscious, but the type of conscious state that interests philosophers is the state of conscious awareness. The distinguishing feature of this state is held to be its subjectively experienced quality, be it found in a perception, a memory, an intention or a belief. Although these psychological attributes can be manipulated via neurology, it is impossible on present knowledge to locate consciousness in a particular part of the brain; the evidence suggests that it is widely distributed. The subjective nature of conscious experience means that science cannot observe it as it would expect to be able to observe a natural phenomenon. The only observer of her conscious states is the conscious subject.

For a long time cognitivists were able to relegate consciousness since it lacked any obvious function within the computational model. Either it would spontaneously emerge in a sufficiently complex machine or it could be eliminated from discussion on the grounds that it did not emerge in a machine otherwise comparable in cognitive terms with a human being. Put on the defensive by its lack of theoretical focus, cognitive science has been forced to take consciousness seriously; it is no longer allowed to ignore it because it can ignore it. In their attempts to account for subjectivity, cognitivists are expected to engage with philosophers and psychologists who do not share their assumptions. Many philosophers do hold a broadly cognitivist position; some espouse the objective of *naturalizing* the mind, in the sense of bringing it, as a natural phenomenon subject to causal laws, within the domain of empirical science. The assumption that a biological system can in principle be naturalized as a physical system is not challenged within mainstream philosophy, although some philosophers would take issue with the description of a person as a 'biological system'.

Ontology and epistemology

A philosophical investigation of consciousness might begin with *ontology*, a term denoting how things really are as opposed to how they present themselves to us as being. In philosophy a feature of the external world is *real* if it exists independently of minds and the construction they put on it; *realism* is the position according to which there is a world with physical properties existing independently of mental construction. There are many forms of realism and of its opposite, *idealism*. The first step in philosophy is often the appreciation that objects cannot be assumed to exist *as we perceive them* independently of our perception of them. For example, we might assume that all visible objects are coloured, just as we perceive them to be. But colour, as I explain presently, cannot be identified, in a consistent or *lawlike* fashion, with any surface property that an object may possess. Instead it depends on an interaction between the visual system and light reflected from a surface. Objects themselves may be colourless. We can imagine a world of uniform colour, but not a world devoid of colour. So, assuming for the sake of this example that colour is not real, we would have a psychological condition that simply prevented us from conceiving of any object in our world as it is in itself, independently of how it presents itself to us. We might then be led to doubt whether other properties of objects are real, for example hardness and smoothness, which arguably refer to how they *feel* to us. Finally we might doubt whether the individuality of objects is real: the division of the world into discrete objects might also be an imposition of our psychology. We might believe that there is something out there, but that nothing can be said about it that does not implicate our cognitive relation to it. To the idealist this implies that the external world, in any form meaningful to us, is *mind-dependent*. This does not prevent the idealist from believing that there is an external reality 'behind' the world of appearances.

Science has encouraged realism by explaining the behaviour of objects with reference to universal laws, which appear to operate unaffected by observation, at least above the quantum level. Science might therefore provide a general criterion of ontology: a phenomenon will be real if it is capable of making a difference in observable, lawlike physical terms, in other words if it has causal efficacy. If its causal effects can be attributed entirely to its *constituent parts*, the phenomenon itself will not be real. It will be instead a convenient construct for the purpose of our dealings with the world. Take the example of a river. We might observe its causal effects in transferring objects from one place to another or in driving machinery that has been placed in its way. But these effects can be attributed to the causal properties of water itself. Moreover, the river's water is completely replaced over a certain period; ontologically the river does not remain identical with itself. Although it could not properly be said to have causal efficacy, it suits us to give it a name and accept it as a permanent feature. Because it does not have a continuous ontological existence, we refer to it as an *epistemological* phenomenon. Epistemological phenomena are mind-dependent. This is not to say that the river is not real, since it consists of something that may well be real.

At this point we can see how the interests of science and philosophy might diverge. For science what matters is the ability to predict the behaviour of observable phenomena on the basis of formulated laws. It has no interest in what cannot be observed. But for the philosopher observation necessarily involves at least an element of mental construction. So there is a question to be asked that does not concern science, namely: what is *really* going on out there, behind what is mentally constructed or epistemological? Despite its triumphant progress, science itself lacks the means to satisfy us that it can, or could ever, answer that question. Of course philosophy may not be able to answer it either.

Although science can generally rely on causation, it remains a highly problematic concept. One difficulty is that if we try to specify the causes of an event, such as the collapse of a building, we find not only that they have previous causes stretching back into the past but also that we cannot exclude from a complete picture such negative causes as a construction fault resulting from an oversight on the part of the project manager, who happened to be distracted by the scene outside his window. When we have finally laid out the causes of the event, we find that they are so specific that they could never be repeated. But the practical interest of causation, especially to science, is that it can be used to extrapolate regularities or laws that allow us to go on to make and test predictions. When we extrapolate, however, there is inevitably an element of epistemological construction on our part. This raises the question, to which I return in Chapter 3, of whether laws of nature are mind-independent. A connected issue is determination. When we have found the causes of an event, is it ever justifiable to claim that, given the presence of those causes, the effect was bound to follow? How could this be required other than by a law, but how could something as general as a law describe the particular circumstances in question? If an event in which causation is evident takes place only once, how could it be an instance of the operation of a law?

Causation takes different forms: a distinction can usefully be made between *linear* and *constitutive* causation. Linear causation describes the interaction of distinct entities, such as billiard balls on a table; constitutive causation denotes the relation of higher-level properties to lower-level organization or microstructure. Thus a piece of metal will be more or less malleable, depending on its properties at a microstructural level. The microstructure of a substance can be altered, for example by heat. Liquidity and solidity are higher-level properties of water at different temperatures. Ice is constitutively caused by the arrangement of H_2O molecules, which slide over one another when water is liquid but form a lattice-like structure when it freezes. The properties of liquidity and solidity cannot be predicted from the hydrogen and oxygen atoms in isolation. They nevertheless qualify as ontological since they are causally efficacious: water can drive a mill and ice can support skaters. Because science will always look for causal efficacy at the lowest observable level of organization, the ontological status of such higher-level properties as liquidity and solidity is specially designated as *emergent*.

The mind–body relation

The problem of the mind–body relation is often characterized in terms of ontology. At first sight subjective mental states seem capable of observable causal efficacy. We make conscious decisions from which physical effects follow in a seemingly causal way. I might form a conscious intention to get a glass of water and then proceed to walk towards the kitchen. But since conscious states cannot be observed by scientific means, they cannot have observable causal effects, produced according to laws of nature. If a physical event is the effect of a conscious state, it must have occurred without an observable cause. Such an occurrence is disallowed on the premise that the physical universe is causally closed, in other words that an alteration to its state must be traceable to an internal cause. This restriction applies to the brain considered as a physical entity and therefore appears to rule out the possibility that conscious states could causally affect it and through it the body. We can observe correlations between subjects' reported conscious states and brain activity, but from this data we cannot infer that conscious states cause brain activity rather than vice versa.

Because the mind is unitary, it might be tempting to suppose that it presents an example of emergence, constitutively caused by the physical microstructure of the brain. But this simply transfers the problem: the mind as a whole, or some emergent component of it, would have to have observable causal efficacy comparable with the solidity of ice. There is no more likelihood of this being found at a macro level than at the level of the simple conscious state. Nothing about the mind as we understand it indicates that it acquires real or observable properties as it upwardly emerges. By contrast the emergent formation of ice can be observed at every stage.

These difficulties can be avoided by treating subjective mental states as nothing more than physical states of the brain. This position, known as *physicalism* or *materialism*, is assumed by cognitivism but predates the computer. It views the physical brain as a causal engine responsive to physical inputs. It allows for mental states to be identified with physically emergent brain states. There may even be emergent brain states not yet properly understood by science, which extend across the cerebrum. These states might in the future be empirically observable, have causal efficacy and correlate with reported mental experiences. However, no amount of physical emergence could overcome the improbability of physical stuff entertaining subjectivity. There is here a conceptual obstacle, admittedly greater for some than for others.

Proponents of physicalism tend to argue that the only alternatives to it are *epiphenomenalism*, the view that conscious states are accidental by-products of brain processes serving no purpose, and *dualism*, the view that mind is something quite other than matter, coexisting in parallel with it but lacking a demonstrable connection. Epiphenomenalism has few takers because it seems improbable that something as evolved as consciousness could have no function. Pending a satisfactory account of the otherness of the mental, dualism induces a dispiriting feeling that the philosophy of mind has not advanced significantly since Descartes' classic formulation in the seventeenth century or kept pace with the growth in knowledge of the brain. Each day brings new evidence that mental states *are* (somehow) connected to brain processes. Dualism is now a kind of placeholder for a future refutation of physicalism. Attempts have been made to construct halfway houses. For example, it has been argued that mental states and brain processes are different ways of characterizing the same thing. But if that thing is ontologically unitary, the position collapses to physicalism in some form; if not, dualism is unavoidable. The influence of Descartes persists in both dualism and physicalism because he seminally defined the physical domain in contradistinction to the mental. The physicalist implicitly accepts this division but holds that the mental is reducible to the physical. But even those who reject both dualism and reductivist physicalism are compelled to define their position within a Cartesian frame of reference: there seems to be no other way of approaching the mind–brain relation or indeed the constitution of matter.

A non-physicalist might pitch the mind–body problem in the following way. We can imagine having at some future time a complete knowledge of the neurology of the brain. We might be able to manipulate it to create any conscious effect and accurately to predict neurological patterns from reported conscious states. So one could imagine a future cognitivism being granted scientific credentials. The question 'How do brain processes give rise to subjective experiences?' would have been answered in the sense that the correlations would have been exposed. But would this really be the end of the matter? Would we not still want to know how physico-chemical states *could* give rise to subjective experiences? This would still constitute a qualitative transformation, which no amount of correlation could adequately explain; the explanatory gap would not shrink as we understood more about the physical system. David Chalmers (1996) has influentially characterized this as the 'hard' problem of consciousness; the 'easy' problem, essentially the scientific problem, is to identify the mind–brain correlations. Not all philosophers accept that there is a hard problem if it is not a problem for science.

Neuronal activity

What then are the physical processes that precede conscious experience? The brain and nervous system consist of special cells, called *neurons*, which transmit electrical pulses or *spike*s to one another through connectors called *synapses*. The neuron's receptors are tree-like extrusions called *dendrites*; it sends signals via a single thread-like *axon*, which can be up to a metre long when the neuron is located in the spinal column. This arrangement means that within a region of the brain, containing billions of neurons, no individual neuron is more than a few links from any other; communication within a *population* of neurons is therefore almost instantaneous. Neurons form *afferent* pathways when they are conducting signals to the brain and *efferent* pathways when they are conveying the brain's 'instructions' to the muscles to effect movement or motor behaviour. Motor neurons are found at the end of efferent pathways, in the muscles; receptor neurons in, for example, the sense organs initiate afferent pathways.

Neuron pulses have varying strengths, which create complex knock-on effects including 'feedback loops' affecting neurons which have already emitted pulses. The pulses look as though they could be carrying information but we do not know by what means or in what form it could be encoded. Brain activity is a function of the behaviour both of individual neurons and of entire populations. An analogy is a company that has just received an unusually large order. It is galvanized at the macro level towards a single, instantly disseminated objective, while at the micro level its employees carry on more or less as normal. Their interrelationships may be put under pressure but their pattern of activity does not substantially change. However they can all be seen to contribute to the collective goal, which at the macro level is something completely new. The company is able to adapt successfully to the challenge, even though this takes a form it could not have precisely foreseen.

If we imagine the company as somewhat unfocused when business is slack, we have an approximation to the state of *chaos* which Walter Freeman (2001) has discovered to be the default for neuron populations. The distinctive feature of chaos, known as 'sensitivity to initial conditions', is that barely perceptible variations in input can ripple or cascade through the system to produce huge variations in output. This idea is commonly expressed by the image of the butterfly that flaps its wings in Brazil and sets off a tornado in Texas. If evolution has organized the brain in such a way that conscious states co-vary with the finest of alterations to the physical substrate, it might be easier to explain how consciousness effortlessly refreshes itself despite constantly changing external conditions and adjustments to body orientation.

Neuronal chaos would be at odds with conventional computation, which requires a stable environment in which symbols retain their values and linear causation is protected; linear processes cannot survive chaos. In his research on the olfactory system of rabbits, Freeman found that repeated instances of the same sensory stimulus did not produce any observable consistency at the neuronal level. If information were being encoded, invariance would be expected. Neural-net computation does not rely on symbolic transformation and may therefore appear to be less vulnerable to Freeman's point. But the organization of a neural net is not chaotic and no one has proposed that its limitations could be addressed by making a chaotic version. On the contrary they are normally highlighted by comparison with symbolic computation.

Phenomenal consciousness

The fact that rabbits have a brain and nervous system might be taken to indicate that they have conscious experience. David Hume had this to say in (1739-40):

> This doctrine ["that beasts are endow'd with thought and reason as well as men"] is as useful as it is obvious, and furnishes us with a kind of touchstone by which we may try

every system in this species of philosophy [theories of mind]. 'Tis from the resemblance of the external actions of animals to those we ourselves perform that we judge their internal likewise to resemble ours; and the same principle of reasoning carry'd one step farther will make us conclude that since our internal actions resemble each other, the causes from which they are deriv'd must also be resembling. When any hypothesis, therefore, is advanc'd to explain a mental operation which is common to men and beasts, we must apply the same hypothesis to both; and as every true hypothesis will abide this trial, so I may venture to affirm that no false one will ever be able to endure it. (1.3.16)

Since Hume there has been evolutionary biology. It can be integrated with his Touchstone to produce the principle that if a characteristic whose outline is common to both humans and other animals can be explained as an evolutionary adaptation, this will defeat any competing explanation. The Touchstone can also be used to support the claim that an animal whose behaviour is affected in a similar way to ours by what in our case would be a conscious experience is likely also to be subject to a conscious experience. I follow Antti Revonsuo (2006) in distinguishing *phenomenal* from *reflective* consciousness. Phenomenal consciousness, sometimes referred to as *sentience*, is the immediate result of sensory input, although it is also active in dreams and can be illusory, while reflective consciousness is the medium in which we think, believe and intend. Animals with neural systems react to external sensory stimuli in a similar way to us, but there is no evidence of belief or intention among other animals that cannot be explained as instinctive. We on the other hand are able to form beliefs and intentions whose content bears no reference to our personal or evolutionary history. We also have self-awareness. The distinction between phenomenal and reflective consciousness could therefore be a way of isolating the element we share with other animals from the element unique to us, on the assumption that other animals possess consciousness in some form.

This is often disputed. The brain absorbs and deals with far more sensory information than it presents to consciousness, so it must be possible for an animal or a person to register a sensory stimulus without experiencing it consciously. It is conceivable that the brain originally functioned in this way and that animals exist today whose brains have not evolved to provide conscious experience. Plants obviously are not conscious but this does not prevent them from reacting to environmental variables like sunlight and registering and repairing damage. On the computational view, consciousness emerges when a brain-like system reaches a certain level of organization; by implication a rudimentary brain could lack consciousness. Neither is it self-evident that phenomenal can be decoupled from reflective consciousness. Sentience is believed by some philosophers to presuppose, in addition to sensation, an awareness *that*, for example that the thing one is looking at is yellow or that one is feeling pain. It can then be argued that the capacity for awareness-that is restricted to beings in possession of reflective consciousness.

Even if the principle of animal sentience is conceded, there will be little agreement about where or how to draw the line between sentient and non-sentient creatures. Of course the phenomenal experience of other animals is unlikely to resemble ours. As an adaptation, it would be focused in ways appropriate to the particular requirements of its owner and consonant with its physiology. Without the reflective element, it would lack the kind of significance with which thought can invest it.

Our willingness to attribute consciousness is arguably affected by the degree of our empathy with other species. *Caenorhabditis elegans* is a nematode worm that measures 1.3 mm, lives in soil and is, together with the fruit fly, the doyen of the laboratory because its systems perfectly balance complexity and tractability. It has a simple brain and nervous system consisting of 302 neurons with some 7000 synapses and sense organs that respond to touch, smell, taste and temperature, if not light. It has two nerve cords running the length of its body near the surface. If we were to grant *C. elegans* sentience, we would presumably not begrudge it to any creature with a nervous system. Its phenomenal experience, if it has any, will certainly not be rich, judged by our standards. But there is no reason why it should be rich if it is functional. Moving to the bottom of the animal scale, we find the single-cell amoeba. It lacks a nervous system but proteins on its surface can sense nutrients and stimulate it to behave appropriately. Like a plant, it is receptive to external conditions. It is, however, part of the meaning of sentience that it should depend on a nervous system.

Sentience attribution poses a version of the 'hard' problem. If *C. elegans* is sentient, this is a fact about the natural world. We might therefore expect science to be able to pronounce on the matter. The issue is after all substantial: it would bear, for example, on our moral responsibility towards other species, if we considered the infliction of pain to have moral significance. But how could science establish whether the worm has sentience? Its behaviour is so different from ours that it cannot be interpreted comparatively, as can the behaviour of fish. J. I. Johnson and A. Åkerman (1998) found that trout which had observed fights between other trout settled their own contests with observed fighters more quickly than those with unfamiliar opponents.

Evidence that *C. elegans* may be sentient has been produced by Shawn Xu and colleagues (Li, 2006), although this was not their aim. They identified a receptor neuron in *C. elegans* containing an ion channel protein, TRP. This afferent neuron is sensitive to stretch in the worm's lateral muscles and therefore provides it with a form of *proprioception* – an animal's awareness (sentient or otherwise) of the position and movement of its own body. When the TRP channel was turned off, the worm's movements became markedly more sinuous so that its locomotion was impaired. The team concluded that under normal conditions the receptor neuron guides muscle movement. It may be significant that TRP channel proteins are also found in humans. We tend to think of consciousness as highly evolved but it may be the simplest way to optimize an activity like locomotion through soil.

Our brains have probably been accumulating adaptations from the time of our earliest neuronally endowed ancestors.

According to Paul MacLean's (1973) triune theory, we have a reptilian brainstem and cerebellum, a limbic system shared with other mammals, which is connected to emotion, and a neocortex exclusive to us, which handles language and thought. We share a common ancestor with reptiles, a later one with primates, an even later one with hominids, as well as a much earlier one with *C. elegans*, 35% of whose genes are closely related to human genes. Our brains will retain traits dating back to the first nervous systems. At some historical point, in one of the common ancestors, the first version of phenomenal consciousness will have appeared. If it first appeared in humans, our sentience could only be an evolutionary accident: the potential for sentience would have evolved to an advanced stage for no purpose. Hume's Touchstone would support the contrary thesis that the sensory systems of other mammals (let's conservatively say) evolved with a similar functionality to ours. Larger mammals also appear to possess a psychology of sentience: they anticipate pleasure and pain and adopt attitudes towards them comparable with ours.

Sensorimotor feedback

Here is a theory about how phenomenal consciousness works. We know that neurons in cortex form stable pathways under pressure of habit. Motor neurons form the interface between the brain and the muscles that effect movement. The more frequently an animal repeats a particular motor behaviour, the more firmly its underlying efferent neuronal pattern will become set. The result is that when an adult animal makes a deliberate movement, it turns out to be the movement the animal 'wanted' to make. *There is no reason why this should be the case other than as the result of practice.* Young mammals spend a lot of time practising motor behaviour and hammering out neuronal pathways for use in adult life; it's called play. Human babies, at the beginning of this learning curve, show a characteristic tenacity even though their flailing movements bring little reward. It is not phenomenal consciousness that directs motor behaviour – in that case young animals would not need practice. Instead it acts as a feedback channel appraising the animal of the accuracy of the correspondence between the pre-conscious initiation of the motor behaviour and the resulting movement. Without feedback this accuracy could not be established or maintained. Normally feedback is in real time since it begins to be registered before the deliberate sequence containing a given movement is completed. The continuous adjustment which this enables creates the illusion, in our case, that consciousness is in control. Feedback encompasses both perception and proprioception. Without the latter an animal would lack the means to maintain its balance and streamline its movements.

At first sight perception would appear to be a means of channeling information about the environment independently of the subject's movement. But it is now generally accepted that perception is not simply passive (Noë, 2005). If it were, we would expect to find that sense organs contained only afferent neurons. In fact they contain many efferent neurons, as well as neurons which have both afferent and efferent characteristics. This fact supports the notion that perception is a kind of active sampling, in which the subject brings internal resources to bear. These resources will have evolved as their fruits in keen perception have been selected for. Whether the perceiving animal is stationary or in motion is a superficial distinction. In either case the animal operates on its environment; its attention is an intervention requiring feedback hardly less than a desperate chase after prey. Feedback has the effect of moulding both the springs of motor behaviour relative to its final expression and the modes of cognition relative to the final interpretation of sensory impressions. The learning mind is constantly primed and honed.

Is this picture more appropriate to certain types of animal than to others? Mammals have a wide range of adaptive behaviour, some of it highly sophisticated. But other animals perform operations in which sensorimotor feedback is critical, for example the construction of artefacts such as nests, hives and webs. Effective feedback is possible in very small brains.

A famous experiment was conducted by Benjamin Libet in (1983). It was already known that a 'readiness potential', or preparatory brain state, precedes voluntary motor behaviour in humans by up to a second, according to measurements taken by means of electrodes attached to the scalp. Libet wanted to find out at what point the conscious decision to make a movement is taken, relative to the occurrence of the readiness potential. In order to capture this, he placed his subjects in front of a screen with a revolving spot of light, with electrodes attached to record readiness potential. He asked them to flex their wrists at will over a period and then report the position of the spot when they decided to perform each action. The results indicated that the readiness potential began on average 0.55 of a second before the wrist movement and 0.35 of a second before the conscious decision. Libet's findings have since been confirmed. They imply that when we think we are initiating an instance of motor behaviour, it has already been initiated pre-consciously.

Although Libet could not use animals in his experiment, his research supports the 'sensorimotor feedback theory' outlined above[1]. Even the simplest of behaviours may involve countless neuronally figured motor adjustments. These could not possibly be consciously initiated. Other experiments by Libet (1981) indicate that consciousness takes about half a second to construct perceptual experience from sensory stimuli (by interrupting the process he suppressed the experience). He suggested that in order to discount the half-second delay the mind then refers the experience back in time to the point of (unconscious) reception by the brain. As everyone has no doubt observed, this delay is not adjusted for when pain is caused by penetration of the skin by a sharp object, whereas when pain is superficial, as in a burn, it seems instantaneous, its cause being captured by touch-sensitive neural receptors.

The waking brain receives a constant bombardment of sensory impressions and transforms them into a faultless continuum of conscious experience. We should perhaps not be surprised by the half-second delay. However a question arises.

---

[1] I acknowledge Kevin O'Regan's and Alva Noë's (2001) somewhat different sensorimotor theory of vision.

Why cannot the brain just do what it needs to do? Why is cumbersome consciousness necessary? The brain could take incoming impressions, process them in a fraction of the time taken to generate conscious experience and provide itself with feedback. David Milner and Melvyn Goodale (1995) found evidence that part of the brain does just that. It has two distinct but interacting ways of processing visual information: the ventral stream is associated with the inferior temporal cortex and linked to conscious awareness, while the dorsal stream is associated with the posterior parietal cortex and linked to finely adjusted motor behaviour. An experimental subject with ventral occipital damage was unable to judge the appearance of objects but was able to catch a ball, while a subject with optic ataxia, involving damage to the dorsal stream, could accurately report on the appearance of objects without being able to reach out and grasp them. In unimpaired subjects Milner and Goodale found that a susceptibility to optical illusion co-existed with motor behaviour that indicated an ability to 'see through' the illusion. They concluded that the demands of visuomotor guidance were sufficiently at variance with those of conscious awareness to have produced parallel systems. If conscious awareness with its enormous processing burden is not required for visuomotor guidance, resources can be concentrated on providing greater motor accuracy more quickly.

The sensorimotor feedback theory is therefore open to the objection that motor control does not depend on phenomenal consciousness. It should be noted, however, that it is intended to explain how visuomotor accuracy is developed and maintained: without the phenomenal element there would be a gradual loss of accuracy. Nevertheless the activity of the ventral stream indicates that a further purpose is being served. Milner and Goodale associate it with object recognition and reasoning in humans. Animals in general are able to recognize and make fine judgements about recurrent features of their environments. We might say that they are able cognitively to *parse* their external world and thereby to assimilate to it more effectively. They recognize predators, members of their own species and food sources. They skillfully negotiate their local landscapes. Again, an amoeba might be said metaphorically to parse its environment when it senses a food source, but I want to define parsing as a cognitive operation reliant on the brain. It should be understood as more than simply object recognition. Not only is the organism equipped to make creative guesses when faced with unfamiliar objects, parsing denotes a receptive stance towards its entire visual field, where the distance and speed of objects may be highly relevant to the animal's interests.

Parsing is preceded by the established phenomenon of *binding*. The brain receives different types of input in respect of the position, size, shape, motion, colour, smell, etc. of a given sensible object. This disparate information is processed in various parts of the brain, which succeeds in synthesizing what is needed to create the awareness of a discrete, persisting entity – the perceived object. This combinatorial process is in the early stages of being understood. Its philosophical significance is that the *percept* of an external object – the consciously experienced end result of the neurological binding process – should be distinguished from the object itself.

The inherence of meaning

If consciousness is evolutionarily optimal, this fact does little to relax the parsimony with which science approaches the question of non-human sentience. Scientific enquiry starts with the physical datum: the brain and nervous system. How these generate consciousness is a mystery. Because it is a scientific mystery, consciousness as an evolutionary fact can be sidelined. At the same time most philosophers discuss the mind without reference to biology, still less evolutionary biology, where important questions remain unsettled. This is especially true in what is known as analytic philosophy, which dominates the Anglo-Saxon academy, the reason being that it cannot countenance dependence on any kind of mediate theory. The exception is Newtonian mechanics, which for some reason is treated as fundamental. Moreover the Cartesian legacy and the success of empirical science discourage philosophical curiosity about biology. Philosophers of biology are primarily concerned with explicating the conceptual framework. Among the few eminent analytic philosophers open to distinctively biological modes of thought is John Searle; it is no coincidence that his name occurs frequently in these pages. The name Daniel Dennett will be raised in objection. Dennett is interested in evolutionary biology but he approaches it as a combative physicalist.

Searle's most famous thought experiment is the Chinese Room (1980). Inside it is a solitary individual who receives a series of messages through a small opening. The messages are in Chinese, a language of which he is entirely ignorant. But, by using a set of rules provided, he can look up the symbols contained in the messages and construct appropriate responses. Viewed from the outside, the Room could contain a person who understood Chinese. In fact there is no understanding – parsing is being carried out by means of the application of the rule set. Because understanding links to meaning, the responses from the Room are not *meant*. Searle is here attacking the idea that a threshold exists above which machines should be considered to have cognitive capabilities like ours – to understand and to mean. The assumed existence of this threshold has provided AI with a tangible goal. Alan Turing had proposed a test for aspiring machines, based on whether or not they could, like the Chinese Room, give a convincing show of understanding. Searle's case is that there is something more to the point than a convincing show, that there is a difference between what happens in the Room when its occupant understands and when he does not understand Chinese, and that this difference is the true threshold separating any computational 'mind' from ours. Searle's challenge to computational cognitivism is to explain how understanding and meaning inhere in the mind if they are as inessential as the Chinese Room, and by implication cognitivism, suggest.

This imaginary scenario exposes three further points. First, it is not disputed that computationalism relies on the mind's having infallible access to internally held rules for symbolic transformation. With a strange perspicuity (there is no reason to believe that he had computational theory in mind) Ludwig Wittgenstein in the *Philosophical Investigations* (1953) confuted the notion that the mind could know what to do next by consulting its own internal rules. Secondly, the man in the Chinese Room can deal successfully with the incoming messages only insofar as the rules have been adequately framed in advance. But many of the impressions received by the brain bear little relation to those previously encountered. It succeeds in assimilating them with ease; at the level of perception, apart from optical illusion, it never shows any sign of being unable to compute. Thirdly, Turing's proposal smacks of behaviourism, according to which mental phenomena must be understood in terms of their related behaviour. After his death, behaviourism was discredited and largely disappeared in name. In fact it survives in the cognitivist assumption that consciousness could in principle be attributed to a machine displaying sufficiently convincing behaviour. A typical reply to Searle involves taking the 'behaviour' of the Room as the primary fact. Since this would be the same whether or not the man inside understood Chinese, the issue of meaning can be made to disappear.

There is a deep division between those who believe that meaning can be eliminated and those, like Searle, who believe that in some important way it resists elimination. The latter would argue that it does not and cannot be made to inhere in a non-biological physical system such as that of a computer, any more than it can be made to inhere in a chunk of silicon. Computers do meaningful things but their function is to create meaning *for us*, in ways that save us time or divert us. Lacking in the debate, however, is a satisfactory theory of meaning. Such a theory would need to distinguish between meaning as real and meaning as epistemological: computers provide us with epistemological meaning without having real or inherent meaning. The Chinese Room also provides epistemological meaning (to someone familiar with Chinese); whether it has inherent meaning depends on whether the man inside the Room understands Chinese. In other words it depends on a fact about a biological system. My purpose in this chapter is to sketch out a biological theory of meaning. Although it is intended to explain the mechanisms of epistemological meaning, it is primarily a theory of ontology.

The S-axis introduced

If it is an adaptation, consciousness may share properties with other adaptations more amenable to investigation. Underlying all of them is the duality of *genotype* and *phenotype*. The genotype is the sum of chemically encoded instructions present in every cell of the organism; the phenotype is the realization of the genotype's instructions in the shape of the organism as an adapted and adaptive unit with a functioning array of phenotypic features or characters. The phenotype is the testing-ground of adaptation whereas the genotype is its power-house. In the case of a phenotypic character like a giraffe's neck, a complex of genes may be responsible. They will have spread in the giraffe population owing to the selective advantage of the phenotypic character for which they are responsible.

Now that we have a complete map of the human genome, we can in principle account for the human phenotype with reference to the human genotype. This is being repeated for other organisms. Science is satisfied with the correlations of the two types of observable phenomenon and assumes a causal relationship between genes and their phenotypic expression. But I suggest there is another explanatory gap, an echo of the 'hard' problem. How is it possible that genes should give rise to phenotypic characters at all? We are not talking simply of the emergence of properties such as solidity, but of form and function. Genes are more than just constitutively causal of phenotypic characters – they *specify* them. But nothing about the genes for a giraffe's neck representationally betrays the fact that they are the genes for its neck rather than its tail. Genes are also causally insufficient in an important way: they presuppose the incorporation of external factors, especially nutrients, to create their phenotypic effects. Genes are contributory causes in a process that remains open.

A different kind of causation operates in the reverse direction, from phenotype to genotype. It is historical and cumulative: as evolution has occurred, the lengthening neck of the giraffe has been accompanied by the development of particular genes in a particular complex. There is a correlation between the neck, on which selection has operated, and these particular genes. There is a relationship of necessity: the giraffe's neck has necessitated and continues to necessitate a particular complex of genes. No event can be isolated as a cause of these genes, neither have they been caused by the neck itself; instead we could say that the evolutionary history of the phenotypic character and its adaptive success are the *reason* for their existence.

We therefore have a bivalent relationship in which qualified forms of causation reinforce each other. Compare the constitutive causation of inorganic microstructures: there is no evolutionary feedback creating selective pressure and therefore no power at the lower level to influence higher-level form. A molecule of gold does not influence the size or shape of the coin or bar containing it.

Let's now look at the giraffe in action. Thanks to its neck it is able to reach higher leaves than other herbivores. It is free to eat leaves at any height it chooses, but there is something non-contingent about its consumption of high leaves, something built into its physiology. Is there a causal relationship? The length of the giraffe's neck contributes to its eating of the high leaves but we would hesitate to say that it causes it. We would have difficulty explaining the difference in causal terms between its eating high leaves and preferring tastier low leaves. Conversely we might wish to say that the length of the giraffe's neck has been caused by evolutionary selection, associated with the consumption of high leaves, that the eating of high leaves has necessitated, or is the reason for, its long neck.

Some phenotypic characters are internal organs. The heart is a contributory cause of the pumping of blood, but this complex process depends on other factors such as the healthy state of blood vessels and indeed the presence of blood. In this case the organ cannot be put to a purpose other than that for which it is adapted.

The pumping of blood has necessitated the heart in the particular form it takes in any given animal. Yet other phenotypic characters are inactively functional: the carapace may regulate body temperature or provide camouflage. There appears to be a bivalent relationship between the phenotypic character and the role for which it is adapted, not unlike that operating between genotype and phenotype. I suggest there is a common factor. As it does not have a name, I'll call it S for now and schematize it by terming the contributory cause the *satisfaciend* and the evolutionary cause the satisfaciend's *condition of satisfaction*. Thus the phenotypic character is the condition of satisfaction of the genes that specify it as functional satisfaciends. At the same time the phenotypic character is itself a satisfaciend with a function: its condition of satisfaction describes its function. The condition of satisfaction of the giraffe's neck is the eating of the high leaves, of the heart the pumping of blood, of the sheep's fleece the maintenance of body temperature.

'Condition of satisfaction' is not my expression; it is normally found in connection with *intentionality*, especially in the writings of Searle (1983). This word is derived from the Latin *intendere*, to stretch forth. It was coined by mediaeval philosophers to describe the capacity of the mind to reach out figuratively and grasp external objects. In the modern period it has been adapted to describe the 'aboutness' of conscious mental states. If I perceive, I necessarily have a perception *of* something. If I have a thought or hold a belief, they are necessarily a thought or a belief *about* some object or state of affairs. The most obvious way to characterize this aboutness is in terms of a projection of the mental towards whatever forms its content. Intentionality is also attributed to phenotypic characters: the heart is 'about' the pumping of blood.

Intentionality is an example of a *metaphysical* concept. If the physics of the brain or the heart were exhaustively examined, no aboutness would be found. But this does not entail that intentionality is not real: external reality may comprise features that cannot be accounted for by science and yet are not constructions on our part. Isolating and investigating such features has been the primary task of philosophy. Another metaphysical concept is causation. Although it appears to denote something real and universal, it cannot be observed, as Hume famously pointed out. Science can only identify the regularity with which an event of type A is followed by an event of type B (for example the striking of a match and its combustion), and then seek to explain the association of the two events in a manner bounded by epistemology. What obtains and occurs at the metaphysical or ontological level is a very open question, on which the findings of science have little or no bearing. So in saying that I want to plant the idea that the necessitation of the *S-axis* (of the satisfaciend by its condition of satisfaction) is metaphysical, I am not making a claim in conflict with what we know.

A defect of intentionality is that the mediaeval connotation of a relationship between mental states and external objects has not been repudiated, indeed it has been elaborated with reference to causation. Thus Searle, like many other philosophers, would say that an external object, for example a red car, causes my perception of it and that this causal relationship is an aspect of the intentionality of my perceptual state. He would also say that the car is the condition of satisfaction of my perceptual state. Although I want to adopt the expression 'condition of satisfaction', I need to redefine it. Searle does not say that the red car, as a condition of satisfaction, necessitates my perception of it – necessitation belongs to *my* definition of the condition of satisfaction. In my sense of the expression, an external object cannot be a condition of satisfaction of a mental state, since no external object could necessitate a mental state. To see this, think of the universe before life: there were plenty of objects but none necessitated a mind or a mental state.

The idea that a red car could cause my perception of it introduces a serious problem of circularity (Praetorius, 2007). To be able to cause my perception, the car would have to have a discrete, independent existence, on the principle that a cause must be separate from its effect. Without this condition, the effect could simply be a way of describing (an aspect of) the cause. The problem is how to grant the car an independent existence from my point of view. As already noted, there are strong grounds for supposing that any properties it may appear to have, such as its redness, are constructed by my neurology. The coherence of the car as a unitary object for me is the result of the binding process that has assembled the percept in my consciousness from the barrage of disparate information hitting my visual system. The car only exists for me through the mediation of these complex processes. So it cannot cause those very processes to be set in train. And, distant as it is from me, the car cannot causally affect me in some alternative way that bypasses my cognition.

Organisms as objects are subject to external causal influences of the linear variety; other objects can penetrate their surfaces and do great damage. But they are, in an important sense, discrete systems. Inputs, whether in the form of sensory stimuli or nutrients, are *expected* by satisfaciends; their normal causal powers are transmuted on entry to the system, where they become adjuncts. The brain's chaotic nature would be sufficient to derail a linear causal train entering via the visual system. The idea that an item of digested food could set off a causal train is equally implausible. For want of a better expression, I'll term any input expected by a satisfaciend an *incorporand*.

One way to conceptualize the S-axis is in terms of *teleology*, notwithstanding that it should be treated with caution in biology. The condition of satisfaction is a *telos* or end, towards which the satisfaciend is oriented. The strength and binding quality of this orientation will have been selected for in competition with that of less focused and less potent satisfaciends. The effect is that of an evolutionary forge: evolutionary history is compressed into the dynamic of the S-axis, creating a relation unique to biology. What emerges is meaning and meaning that is real: the satisfaciend *means* its condition of satisfaction.

The brain as satisfaciend

The brain is composed of cells and resembles a physical phenotypic character, specified by the genotype. However, unlike every other such character its physical form does not define its function. Instead it generates the mind. The mind could not be generated straight from the genotype – a physical intermediary is necessitated. But S is indifferent to the number of steps required to achieve an effect. The best example of this flexible dynamic is *gene expression*. DNA is transcribed from its source in genes into messenger RNA, which is translated, with the addition of nutrients, into cellular proteins. Amenable to chemical modification, proteins then provide the building blocks of organs. Each stage is necessitated but should not for that reason be treated as a satisfaciend. Genes may break down into chemical elements with a claim to be *their* satisfaciends, although they are unlikely to qualify. The criteria for a satisfaciend are that it specifies its condition of satisfaction, is not merely a vehicle of antecedent specification and expects incorporands of some kind. The brain qualifies because it expects sensory incorporands.

But what precisely is its condition of satisfaction? Taken in conjunction with the nervous system, it has both afferent and efferent elements. The efferent condition of satisfaction is motor behaviour, including all purposive muscular activity. The afferent condition of satisfaction is more difficult to define. We could use a broad term such as 'cognition' and apply it uncontroversially to all animals with a brain/nervous system. Or we could use a contentious term such as 'consciousness', with the implicit, scientifically unverifiable, claim that all animals with a brain/nervous system are sentient. Given the state of our knowledge, it would probably be sensible to exercise caution in naming the brain's afferent condition of satisfaction.

Although we normally conceive of the mind in its cognitive role, it may be necessary to extend this to include resources essential to purposive motor behaviour. Alternatively, if phenomenal consciousness is a condition of satisfaction of the brain, the mind as an intermediate category may get squeezed, unless it has a distinctive support role or functions analogously with the stages of gene expression. The relationship of brain to consciousness is no more radically transformative than that of genotype to phenotype. We accept the latter as unremarkable because each category is empirically observable, they appear to correlate and a causal relation can be assumed. Science requires nothing more. Similarly the brain's production of motor behaviour is transformative yet unremarked. Its production of conscious experience is of a kind with other S-mediated processes and only appears to be exceptional because conscious experience is private. But this just would be the case. The fact that conscious states are only available to their subjects does not mean that the brain-consciousness axis ceases to be ontological and becomes semi-epistemological. Nor does the fact that only a mind can appreciate biological function entail that it is epistemological.

Biological function and meaning are therefore to be regarded as mind- or observer-independent; this remains the case when meaning is cognitive and assumes the quality of subjectivity. Searle is therefore correct in maintaining that there is no reason why subjectivity should not be ontological and amenable to science provided the appropriate tools are available. Unfortunately it is difficult to imagine such tools becoming available. But this does not invalidate the point.

A key distinction should be made between the *expressed* meaning of the satisfaciend and the complementary *realized* meaning of the condition of satisfaction. When I say that the condition of satisfaction of the giraffe's neck is the eating of high leaves, I describe the expressed meaning of a functional satisfaciend, as it presents itself to the observer. Meaning is realized when the satisfaciend finds its condition of satisfaction in the actual eating of particular high leaves. There is thus a counterpoint between epistemology and ontology: we understand a real biological function by observing its instrument at rest. The position can also be analyzed by distinguishing two S-axes: firstly that between the giraffe's physiology and its foraging behaviour and secondly a cognitive S-axis from the giraffe's neck to the observer's recognition of its function.

If S is real, it may have implications for cognitive science, whose programme involves uncovering physically observable phenomena which correlate sufficiently with conscious states to provide the basis for a predictive science in the conventional sense. The search is for what are termed the *neural correlates of consciousness*. This could mean either a functional correlation with, for example, the neural activity responsible for the colour element of the binding process or a strict correlation between neural activity and phenomenal content – the objects that populate our visual experience. On the computational model, all phenomenal content will either stand in a causal relation to a particular neuronal state or will be identified with it. Suppose that Mary is seated in front of a screen which regularly switches colour through red, yellow, blue and green. Computational cognitivism expects to find neural correlates of Mary's conscious experience such that by looking inside her brain it can tell which colour the screen is at any moment. Conversely, when the screen is yellow, it hopes to predict occurrences in her brain absent when the screen is blue. As neuroscience advances, evidence will be sought for correlations between neuronal states and the perceptual experience of particular yellow objects.

Physical phenotypic characters are permanent and have permanent genetic satisfaciends. Satisfaciends correlate with their conditions of satisfaction and vice versa. I did not need to say 'and vice versa' since correlation is bi-directional. The genome map documents the correlation of genotype and phenotype. Conscious states by contrast are ephemeral. This creates a difficulty for S-theory: necessitation must travel down from ephemeral conscious states to the brain so as to be specified at the physical level. But the number of neurons is finite, while the number of possible conscious states is infinite. Neurons must be reuseable for the production of future conscious states. They must therefore be to some degree independent of the conscious states to which they contribute and which they survive. In this respect they resemble computer memory. But if they do not specify particular conscious states, they cannot be necessitated in the correlative sense required by S.

One of two conclusions follows. Either S is absent from the process and meaning can survive a contingent relation between neurons and the information they carry (the computational model) or conscious states correlate with something other than neurons. But how could necessitation *not* travel down through neurons when they are what the brain consists of? Here I believe we come to the heart of the evolutionary matter as far as the brain is concerned. An adaptation was required that could conduct necessitation from ephemeral states *via an ephemeral medium* to a permanent physical organ. In the firing of neurons we witness the transition from the permanent to the ephemeral. The firings are perfectly observable, although we may not yet be very good at observing them. A physicalist might argue that conscious states are nothing more than such firings, which takes us straight back to the hard problem. S however extricates us from this all too familiar corner by allowing us to hypothesize a further transformative relation between mass firings and conscious states, in which causation is weak and meaning is preserved and realized. Conscious states initially necessitate and correlate with mass neuronal firings, which are also infinite. In some way necessitation continues down to the permanent brain, which lacks the physical definition found in other parts of the body.

The question for cognitive neuroscience is whether to limit investigation to functional correlation or to pursue content-specific correlation between neuronal and conscious states. Genotype/phenotype correlation is forged when evolutionary selection has a chance to operate on inter-generationally stable phenotypic features. Selection can operate on conscious functions, which are known to correlate with types of neuronal activity in specific regions of the brain, but it cannot operate on unrepeatable conscious states. There could therefore be no evolutionary pressure on content-specific neuronal states to be sufficiently invariant to support a predictive model.

Phenotypic plasticity

Giraffes not only have a long neck, they also have long legs and a suitable torso. Phenotypic characters are not necessitated in isolation by their conditions of satisfaction: the entire phenotype is primed to function as a unitary whole. Selection will not only have ironed out conflicts between the functions of phenotypic characters: it will, where possible, have enhanced those functions with the aid of other characters. This is especially true when the animal has adapted to a niche that can be defined with reference to the function in question. The giraffe's niche comprises uncontended access to certain vegetation within a certain type of ecosystem.

It may be possible to draw a parallel with consciousness. Although this would be difficult to demonstrate, it may be the case that its seamless unity relies on a form of systemic streamlining, in which disparate brain activity conduces to the most beneficial conscious effect at any given moment with distraction kept to a minimum. What we experience as coherence, which gives rise to the concept of the unitary self, may be a lack of interference from sources of functional conflict.

This would depend on *phenotypic plasticity*. The conjunction of genetics and evolutionary biology in the mid-twentieth century encouraged the view that evolution proceeds as minute, random genetic variations produce correspondingly minute, random alterations at the phenotypic level, on which selection can operate. It was always going to be difficult to explain how phenotypic alteration of this kind could have a net benefit at every stage. The explanation was bound to implicate developmental biology, with which evolutionary biology came to terms in the 1990s in a field known as 'evo-devo'. Among its concerns are the extremely complex mechanisms that regulate the stages of gene expression. Under one aspect these are highly conservative – the basic vertebrate body plan, for example, has not changed for 500 million years. But, as Marc Kirschner and John Gerhart (2005) explain, this core conservatism goes hand in hand with regulated *deconstraint* at more superficial levels. Small genetic variations need not be immediately expressed in phenotypic variation but may instead be buffered in such a way that they help to optimize future alterations to the phenotype. The effect is a bias towards viability in phenotypic variation, on which selection has operated to produce the enormous variety of vertebrate forms.

If the variations thrown up by regulated deconstraint were on balance less viable, the system itself would be selected against – it is an axiom of evo-devo that selection does not operate solely on phenotypic characters. So a key aspect of regulation is the beneficial synthesis of the diverse array of specificatory pressures at work within a given phenotypic feature. Arkhat Abzhanov and colleagues (2004) examined beak development in several species of Darwin's finches living on the Galapagos Islands and found that differences correlated with levels of a growth factor protein, Bmp4, produced by neural crest cells in the birds' heads. When they introduced Bmp4 into the neural crest cells of chicken embryos, they developed larger beaks similar to those of the ground finches. Significantly, the form of the chickens' heads modified itself to accommodate the larger beak and obviate a deformity. In other words, a regulatory mechanism was triggered which optimized the outcome across a larger and more complex system than that responsive to the level of Bmp4.

Plasticity is essential to sexual reproduction, every instance of which gives rise to a unique combination of genetic material. As a rule, this progeny is not merely viable in the harsh circumstances it finds itself facing, but perpetuates uncompromised adaptive functionality. When a Great Dane mates with a poodle, the result is likely to be a rounded, healthy animal. As Kirschner and Gerhart put it, the organism is a poised response system; it responds to mutation creatively by virtue of *expectant* mechanisms operating within certain customary boundaries. Although the evolution of species is not fully understood, it is noteworthy that speciation serves to limit the degree of accommodation required.

Plasticity characterizes both internal mechanisms and the outward orientation of the organism towards a variable environment. Because they are stationary, plants are especially vulnerable to changes in temperature and shortages of nutrients. They may adjust by altering their phenotypes, for example by shedding their leaves. Animals have different options, such as migration, but they cannot always evade unwelcome environmental features: the North American snail develops a thicker shell when the threat of predation from crabs is present. Outward plasticity is based on a settled repertoire of responses, none of which is novel. Evolutionary theory does not allow an organism to throw up a phenotypic response to environmental conditions which is at once genuinely new and beneficial, unless this happens by chance. But it is clearly difficult for the biologist to define what is genuinely new, when the phenomenon in question may break down into the subtlest of reactions to the minutest of environmental factors, with plasticity promoting adaptive coherence at every formative stage.

Under exceptional conditions, such as when a population is displaced from its niche or when niches become vacuums, as after the extinction of the dinosaurs, the mechanisms of gene expression may be so disturbed by environmental change and the demands of outward plasticity that they throw up phenotypic alterations. These will form around habitual responses to familiar aspects of the new environment. In this sense they will not be novel. But if the new environment is radically different, it may provoke a synthesis of disparate responses that arguably constitutes genuine novelty. Given the manner of its production and the optimizing balm of plasticity, this novelty is likely to be beneficial; it would only need to be slightly beneficial to be selected for. All this without genetic variation.

Evolutionary selection can only operate on characteristics that remain stable between generations. On the traditional view, such characteristics would be genetically specified. Eva Jablonka and Marion Lamb (1995), however, describe several examples of *epigenetic* inheritance systems, in which phenotypic variation is linked to regulatory expression rather than to genetic variation. All the cells of an organism contain the same genetic information. But when specialized cells such as liver or kidney cells divide, the daughter cells are of the same type. Specialization is linked to the switching on or off of genes: the switch settings can be transmitted along with the 'neutral' genetic information. When a female horse is crossed with a male donkey, the result is a mule, but when a male horse is crossed with a female donkey, the result is a hinny. Hinnies and mules differ phenotypically but are genetically identical. This can only be explained if their genes are in some way tagged as having been inherited from the father or the mother.

The organism's contingent, multi-layered relationship with its environment makes possible other approaches to heritable, non-genetic phenotypic variation. Matteo Mameli (2004) has a thought experiment featuring a hypothetical species of butterfly. It has evolved to lay its eggs on a particular plant: when a female caterpillar hatches, it imprints on the taste of the plant's leaves, leading it to select by taste the same plant when laying its own eggs as a butterfly. Mameli introduces the 'lucky butterfly', which, owing to a developmental accident affecting the imprinting mechanism, lays her eggs on a different plant, which has been recently introduced into the butterflies' environment. As it happens, this plant suits the development of caterpillars of the species better than the customary plant: the butterfly offspring of the lucky mother are bigger and therefore fitter than normal. But because their imprinting mechanisms do not malfunction, their offspring imprint on the new plant. After several generations, their success leads to all members of the species being bigger and hatching on the new plant. Because the phenotypic alteration is intergenerationally stable, evolutionary selection can operate on it but, crucially, there need have been no genetic variation. Such shifts may well have occurred in evolutionary history.

If inherited epigenetic variation is a fact and allows a beneficial novelty to spread through a population, genetic variation can then catch up within the buffer provided and reinforce the adaptation. If the phenotypic variation is environmentally induced, there may be no catch-up. To say that the phenotype correlates with the genotype may be a simplification. It may be due in large part to modes of gene expression with only weak support from genes. The proportion of genes we share with other species indicates that, even when protected by a phenotypic buffer, genetic variation is slow to catch up.

The context in which these developmental processes give rise to beneficial novelty could be described as *teleological chaos*. By this I mean that although the processes are chaotic in character and are typified by weak causal linkage, they do not bring about a random or uncontrollable outcome. Quite the opposite: as a condition of satisfaction, the final adaptation imposes necessitation down through the system to the genetic level, which in turn projects the expectancy of the satisfaciend up through the complex layers of poised chaos. I need hardly add that this is a strictly biological phenomenon. It may have the virtue of defusing combinatorial explosion. Plasticity within the brain is generally identified with the capacity of neurons to form new relationships and pathways. Chaos provides a suitably permissive environment. If the system were teleologically chaotic, this would imply that neural plasticity could remain poised and focused even while generating novelty. In this context novelty will take both afferent and efferent forms. Efferent novelty would describe behavioural adaptation to unfamiliar circumstances, while afferent novelty would denote cognitive adaptation to the perceptually unfamiliar.

When an animal faces its external world, it requires 'complete coverage'. It needs to be actively cognizant of both familiar and unfamiliar features of the environment, even if this leads to occasional mistakes. Without plasticity there would be a bias towards engaging only with the familiar and the expected, the inherent tendency of any 'intelligent' machine. The brain capable of throwing up advantageous behavioural novelty in the form of dependable strategy against the unfamiliar will obviously be selected for. But such novelty need not rely on evolutionary selection to spread through a population: it can be observed and imitated. The advantageous behaviour may then somehow be consolidated as instinct. It is possible that neurology permits a kind of loose linkage between genes and behaviour similar to that created by the regulatory mechanisms between genes and the physiological phenotype. This could mean that some instinctive behaviour is epigenetically 'written away' rather than genetically encoded.

Direct and indirect perception

We are now in a position to look more closely at perception. With the aid of sensory stimuli, the brain provides us with phenomenal experience of the external world. Everything we know about the neurological production of this experience indicates that it is confined to our heads and yet it seems implausible that phenomenal content – the cats, trees and cars that populate our experiences – is so confined. But if these things are outside our heads, how do they end up inside them? I am going to offer a possible route to a resolution of this conundrum.

The standard view in philosophy is that the perceptual world is an internal *representation* of the external world; the objects of perception are surrogates for objects in the world beyond the head. Perception on this schema is *indirect*. The representation is capable of presenting to us the distilled perceptible properties of the external object while concealing any properties of its own. The distilled properties have a cognitive rather than a purely sensational force: the representation is physically realized in the brain as an object of cognition.

Steven Lehar (2003) makes explicit the consequences of the representational view, at least as he sees them. He holds that what we take to be the external world is a model constructed by the brain and contained by the head – a kind of virtual reality in which our own bodies feature. The inner wall of one's skull is therefore beyond everything one can see. To the objection that what we see may be miles or light years away, Lehar replies that the internal model is a volumetric, spatially organized version of external reality, into which perspective is introduced in such a way as to give an illusion of distance (perspective does not exist in the real world beyond the head).

What does the model consist of? When one turns one's head, the model remains stationary, so it cannot be made of permanent brain tissue. Lacking evidence about what it might be constituted of, Lehar's impulse is nevertheless empirical. He assumes that the brain/mind is a physical system and that phenomenal consciousness, which he accepts, must in principle be capable of replication in a machine. The only way to design a conscious machine, he argues, would be to give it an internal model of its external world. The model would be self-presenting in some unspecified way. Phenomenal consciousness should therefore be investigated from the evidence that the practicalities of designing a conscious machine would provide. Lehar admits his theory is incredible, but considers it less incredible than what he takes to be the only alternative, a direct theory of perception.

The type of view espoused by Lehar has traditionally been charged with the *homunculus fallacy*. If the representation is realized inside the head, then it must be perceived, the argument goes, by a subject also located inside the head. While our own sense organs are oriented towards the external world, we might imagine a homunculus or 'little man' sitting inside the head and applying his visual system to the representations it contains. But by the same token, the homunculus himself would require his own internal homunculus to watch the resulting representations inside his (the first homunculus') head. An infinite regress is therefore introduced, which the representationalist must forestall by showing why the homunculus is redundant. But if the representational model is able to present itself to consciousness without the assistance of a homunculus, we have to ask why the external world could not similarly present itself.

Other representational theories reject the notion that when I perceive a red car I have access to something that visually resembles a red car. Fred Dretske (1995) takes as an example the operation of a car's speedometer, which is about the speed at which the car is travelling – a speedometer can have intentionality. Drestke defines representation thus: a system Z represents a property F if and only if Z has the function of indicating (providing information about) the F of a certain domain of objects. Z performs its function by occupying different states corresponding to different determinate values of F. The speedometer represents the speed of the car by providing information to the driver. The state of pointing to 50 when the car is doing 50 mph is a representational fact about the speedometer.

There are facts about the speedometer that are not representational facts, such as its being connected by means of a cable transmitting information about wheel rotation. The difference between representational and non-representational facts is the difference between the mind and the brain. The mind operates by manipulating physically encoded representational facts.

When a person has a conscious phenomenal experience, for example the perception of a red car, Dretske holds that the content of the experience is factive or informational. The subject is aware of the redness of the car, that is, she is aware that the car is red. She registers the redness of the car in the same way that the speedometer registers the speed of the car. This does not involve awareness of something red, any more than that the speedometer displays something travelling fast. The factive content of the perception presents in the subject as a kind of belief. As information it is amenable to being physically encoded and integrated with the rest of the subject's psychology.

It becomes clearer that a theory of representation is really a theory of perceptual meaning and that presentational qualities are those which lend meaning to the perceptual experience. If an experience has meaning for its subject, we can usually depict it factively as meaning *that* something is the case. Representationalism seeks to distil meaning from the presentational character of the experience and hold it at a cognitive level. If this is treated as a conceptual level and concepts are taken to presuppose language, there will be implications for the capacity of animals to have perceptual experiences. The problem is evident in the case of pain. Representationalists disagree about what pain represents and often omit it from their narrative; it would be a weakness of the general theory if it represented nothing. Some hold that it represents itself, others that it represents damage to the subject's body. For animals and very young children it is difficult to see how, from the first-person point of view we are concerned with, pain could represent damage to the body. But to say that pain represents itself looks suspiciously like a way of saying that it represents nothing. So if we believe that very young children can experience pain, the lack of a linguistic-conceptual faculty in other animals should not prevent them from experiencing it too.

To say that pain represents nothing to its subject is not to say that it lacks meaning to its subject. So it may be possible here to drive a wedge between representation and meaning. This would normally be difficult since a theory of meaning independent of a theory of representation would be required; representation would appear to offer the best means of analyzing and elucidating perceptual meaning. My claim, however, is that S promises a general theory of meaning, by which standard the claims of representation can be assessed. As part of the brain's condition of satisfaction, perceptual experience instantiates realized meaning. Plasticity enables a generalized conscious experience in which realized meaning dependent upon a variety of brain functions is merged. This incorporand-acquisitional process integrates binding and parsing before *terminating* in the phenomenal condition of satisfaction; there is no further stretching forth, there is no intentionality. When we project aboutness *from* our conscious states, we misinterpret their final, qualitative, realized but transparent character. We all know what phenomenal experience is like: what it is like is functional realized meaning. This also applies to pain.

In higher animals perception can integrate highly complex cognitive processing. In addition to binding and parsing, it has two further components, which I'll term *focus* and *construal*. Focus allows us to select from the visual field. I might believe and say that I am looking at a red car, but I cannot occlude the rest of my visual field. When I look at a clock, therefore, I bind, parse and focus. I also construe the time to be what the clock indicates it to be. I want to distinguish construal from inference, its rule-based computational equivalent. A robot designed to tell the time would have an internal set of rules against which to process incoming information and then infer the correct time. Representationalism has the merit that it does not necessarily rely on inference but it underestimates the role of the conscious subject in construal. The representation itself does not suffice for meaning, which requires an active subject: by bringing his knowledge to bear, he endows the appearance of the clock with meaning. The fact that my watch says 3.40 can *not* mean (to me) that it is 3.40, if I know it is five minutes fast. While I work out that the time is actually 3.35, I may seem to be making an inference. But, if I am not a robot, there are no grounds for denying that my awareness that it is 3.35 is part of my *perception* of the watch. Dretske would say that my watch misrepresents the time, but it doesn't to me. Again, suppose that, at 3.40, a person is looking at a clock that says 3.40 but in fact, as he knows, stopped yesterday. The representation is true but meaning is absent.

A familiar exhibit in this context is the stick that looks bent because it is half-immersed in water. It presents a problem for representationalism because the perceptual experience represents the stick as being bent without inducing any kind of belief to that effect in a person who knows that the appearance of bentness is explained by optics. The appearance may induce a belief that the stick is bent in a less well-informed person but it is not sufficient to do so. Meaning on the other hand follows the subject's construal of the appearance. It cannot be made to inhere in the representation. The representational function of Dretske's speedometer requires an observer's perceptual construal.

I have already suggested that concepts should be interpreted as pre-linguistic cognitive attributes shared by animals capable of successfully parsing new instances of a class of objects. Construal is similarly intended to denote a cognitive capacity common to other animals. If a cat or dog is watching you pass (with sufficient interest) and its view of you is temporarily obstructed, it will anticipate your reappearance on the other side of the obstruction. If a cat is chasing a mouse and the mouse disappears, the cat will normally look for it. A snake in the same situation will immediately lose interest. The anticipatory reaction of the cat or dog is evidence of construal and of the meaning of the perceptual experience for the animal.

This does not prove that the animal's experience is phenomenal (neither would I wish to deny sentience to snakes). My point is that its attribution cannot be restricted by appeal to a cognitive capacity defined in human terms, when it has clear pre-linguistic antecedents. Construal may help us to understand the evolutionary significance of sentience: it might be the case that only with sentience is construal, as opposed to inference, possible. Inference is potentially conflictive: if a complex perceptual experience were to be processed against two mental attributes, it could produce two conflicting conclusions. By forcing a cognitive outcome at the perceptual stage, sentient construal, aided by plasticity, would have a streamlining effect and reduce pressure on the brain's resources. In a comparable way, sentient parsing may achieve a similar economy in animals whose cognition does not stretch to construal.

As a theory of mind, Dretske's factive representationalism is a form of *externalism*, whose thesis is that mental states are causally individuated by external conditions. S-theory on the other hand takes the brain to be responsible for the constitutive, intrinsic origination of conscious states and is therefore an *internalist* theory. With incorporands in the form of light and sound waves and other inputs collected by the senses, evolutionary pressure has created the situation in which phenomenal consciousness as a whole co-varies with external reality to such a fine degree that there appears to be a lawlike, causal correlation. But if it were the case that external objects set off linear causal trains which penetrated the brain and culminated in corresponding conscious states, at a typical moment a brain would be confronted with the task of dealing with hundreds of such trains. In fact the waking brain is fully stretched in generating phenomenal consciousness by chaotic means, which simply do not support linear causation.

Representational theories of perception assume a physical, non-perceptive 'mediating psychological state'. Only if it were physical could the mediating state be causally individuated. It has form and content: its form is a neural configuration of some kind, its content is derived extrinsically and causally from the relevant external object. I have already mentioned the problem of circularity this poses. On S-theory by contrast perceptual content is intrinsically specified within the satisfaciend/condition of satisfaction axis; external objects and conditions have no causal role, mediating states are redundant, phenomenality is the endpoint of the process and intentionality is a false externalization of realized meaning. S therefore will not support an indirect theory of perception. But if perceptual content must be intrinsically specified rather than extrinsically derived from the external object, a direct theory of perception, assuming this could be coherently stated, would also appear to be ruled out.

This position is not unprecedented. Revonsuo (2006), for example, argues for the existence of a self-presenting phenomenal level in the brain, the culmination of a succession of levels generated by neuronal activity. He does not believe that computation alone is likely to explain the complexity of this rising organization or that the phenomenal level is representational. There is no mediating state. He also rejects direct perception because he takes it to imply that the world is ontologically as we perceive it to be and to discount the constructive role of neurophysiology. Revonsuo's pragmatic model is the most eligible I have found for a 'marriage' with S-theory. He regards consciousness as a real, irreducible biological phenomenon to be investigated by neuroscience and he (tentatively) envisages a future empirical model of consciousness. But the purpose of this model will be to explain consciousness in terms of its *constitutive mechanisms* in the rising levels of organization rather than in terms of its neural correlates. An analogy with the stages or levels of gene expression suggests itself; I would guess that the rising levels of organization are required by the transition from the permanent brain to the ephemeral states of consciousness. Mere correlation between conscious and neuronal states would not for Revonsuo be sufficiently explanatory. As he points out, astronomers were able to discern regularities long before they were able to explain them. He is also realistic about the problems involved when the evidence is so complex and the phenomenon to be explained is private:

> I suspect that it is very difficult to construct a model of the phenomenal level that bears the appropriate similarity

relationships to phenomenal reality, unless the phenomenal level itself is used as the output domain where the model is presented. (p. 347)

I would express the same point by saying that the neurological data may not be meaningful outside the S-axis to which it belongs.

Perception and proprioception

A distinction made by John Locke in (1689) still commands general assent:

> The qualities then that are in bodies rightly considered, are of three sorts:
> First, the bulk, figure, number, situation, and motion or rest of their solid parts. Those are in them, whether we perceive them or no; and when they are of that size that we can discover them, we have by these an idea of the thing as it is in itself, as is plain in artificial things. These I call *primary qualities*.
> Secondly, the power that is in a body, by reason of its insensible primary qualities, to operate after a peculiar manner on any of our senses, and thereby produce in *us* the different ideas of several colours, sounds, smells, tastes, etc. These are usually called *sensible qualities*.
> Thirdly, the power that is in any body, by reason of the particular constitution of its primary qualities, to make such a change in the bulk, figure, texture, and motion of another body, as to make it operate on our senses differently from what it did before. Thus the sun has the power to make wax white, and fire, to make lead fluid. These are usually called *powers*. (2.8.23)

We now know more about the peculiar manner after which sensible qualities are produced in us. The most interesting case is colour. Light is a form of electromagnetic radiation (EM), which can be measured by its wavelength, conventionally in nanometres. At one end of the EM spectrum are radio waves, which can measure over a metre, at the other are x-rays and gamma rays, measuring less than a billionth of a metre. Visible light occupies a range from about 780 nm (0.00000078 metres) to 380 nm and falls into bands corresponding to phenomenal colours. When light contains an equal mix of waves within this range, it appears white. Objects, notably the Sun, can emit EM, or they can reflect it. Depending on their microstructure, they can also absorb light waves in particular ranges. When an object absorbs 'red' and 'blue' wavelengths but reflects 'green', it will appear to us to be green. A white object reflects all wavelengths within the visible spectrum while a black object absorbs all wavelengths. Phenomenal colour results when reflected light waves hit sensitive cells in the retina and are converted to information which passes via the optic nerve to the brain. In the human retina there are some 6 million 'cones' attuned to long, medium or short wavelengths. Within these bands the predominant associated colours are red, green and blue respectively. In some way not entirely understood the cones in combination synthesize determinate colour values. Colour vision will have been selected for because, compared with monochrome vision, it greatly increases an animal's capacity to discriminate and thereby to assimilate to its environments. It is standard in all the major groups of vertebrates and in many invertebrates, notably bees.

It is generally assumed in the empiricist tradition that because all information about the external world reaches us via the senses, our awareness of the primary qualities of objects, such as their shape, must be derived from the impact on us of their sensible qualities. But do we lack any other kind of purchase on the external world? It is easy in this context to underestimate the role of proprioception, the Cinderella of the senses. Its sisters go to the ball and get to dally with external objects. But it has its own story to tell. Imagine you are standing sideways to a wall and trying to raise the arm touching it. If your hand is uncovered, your sense of touch will pick up the wall's surface properties and temperature. But proprioception will tell you something else: that you, as an object occupying space, have met another such object, which you cannot dislodge. In search of a term to express what amounts to more than a sensation, A. D. Smith (2002) borrowed from Fichte the word *Anstoss*, meaning 'push' or 'resistance'.

Proprioceptive *Anstoss* is closely associated with touch, but should be considered apart: a person whose sense of touch had been completely anaesthetized would still be able to register it. Conversely, one might feel a feather against one's skin without proprioception.

Revonsuo has a thought experiment in which he asks us to imagine we are space travellers descending to a strange planet. Because we are not attuned to the planet's peculiar physics, we pick up no information via our sense organs. We see, hear, smell nothing: all is dark and silent. The planet is in fact Earth – the point of the experiment is to challenge our assumptions about direct perception. But although as aliens we would be unable to exercise our sense organs, nothing could prevent us from tripping over things and falling flat on our faces. It is far easier to imagine a scientist manipulating our neurology to produce a visual or touch sensation than an *Anstoss* experience.

William Molyneux put the following question to Locke in 1688. If a man born blind had learned by touch to distinguish a cube and a sphere, would he, on becoming able to see, recognize them by sight? Molyneux's Question created enormous interest at the time; it qualifies as one of history's great thought experiments by still being pertinent. Locke's answer was No; he agreed with Molyneux that the blind man's tactile idea of a cube, having been arrived at by experience, could not instantly be converted to a visual idea. Attempts to answer the Question experimentally have never been conclusive. It is a prerequisite that the man should immediately and confidently 'recognize' the shapes; he is not allowed time to work out what they are. Otherwise it would presumably be like asking a person who had only seen certain recondite shapes at a distance to identify them by touch with his eyes closed, which would no doubt be fairly easy. But no one could be expected to recognize a guava visually after having tasted it, no matter how much time he was given.

This could be taken to indicate that vision is linked cognitively to touch. I suggest that the real connection is with the *Anstoss* and that the modes of perception, as distinct from proprioception, are, as Locke held, independent. We can perhaps surmise that vision in infants develops in conjunction with experience of the *Anstoss*, which unfailingly corroborates the spatial, volumetric disposition of the visual field, helping to create the conviction that, in seeing, we are in direct contact with our surroundings. At the same time vision becomes a reliable guide to primary qualities and has the advantage of stretching colourfully to the horizon. It is more subject than the *Anstoss* to illusion since the brain is under greater pressure to take short cuts when processing visual inputs. The other senses do not provide access to mass and spatial relationships, unless one is a bat.

Proprioceptive *Anstoss* may throw light on perception. It takes a reading from the immediate effect on the organism of an external object. But it can also be exercised remotely via a rigid instrument: eyes closed, one could use a stick to count the number of humps on a camel. Visual and auditory perception takes a reading from the effect of an object on its physical environment, to which the sense organs are also connected. Because water has different properties from air, aquatic animals have a distinctive sensory apparatus. For example, sharks have along their flanks mucus-filled pockets (the *ampullae of Lorenzini*), which are sensitive to electrical disturbances caused by other fish. In the cases of touch and taste, the mediated physical relation collapses to immediate contact between the object and the relevant sense organ. In all cases the subject has a physical link to the experienced object: evolutionary adaptation is a matter of the sensitivity with which the link is primed.

I suggest that proprioceptive experience cannot be given representational character. If I grasp a solid object, its solidity and shape to me are not representational of the object's real solidity and shape. I experience those properties directly; the object presents itself in my consciousness. An object felt by means of a stick stands in the same relation to me, despite my very limited ability to sense its properties. Now imagine vision as a kind of 'remote' proprioception, that is, as an adaptation to the physical mediation of light waves, on the same principle as the mediating stick but refined by evolution to an almost implausible degree. During evolution vision will have outrun the other senses as the optimal mode of self-presentation of external objects. It need not have been vision: hearing has assumed this role in bats. The things we see therefore *are* external objects. Does this mean that we perceive them directly? We could tighten the definition of direct perception, citing the constructive role of neurophysiology and distinguishing the object outside the head from its percept inside, in order to give a negative answer to the question, but, absent a mediating psychological state, it is simply more accurate to say that perception is direct than that it is indirect. The constructive role of neurophysiology is not itself at issue in the debate between direct and indirect theories of perception. However, it may stand in the way of a full-blooded realism in respect of the objects of perception.

I am going to avoid the debate between realism and idealism but I will make one observation. Organisms appear to us to be discrete entities with a continuous existence, but the only evidence we have for this is thought to be the evidence of our senses. If we had ontological evidence for the discreteness of organisms, it would lend weight to realism about such entities and by implication about other entities that appear to us to be discrete. The biological S-axis is always contained by an organism, even by an organism parasitic on another. If the S-axis is ontological, an organism could be defined as possessing S-axes, none of which extends beyond its physiological limits; every ontological S-axis will belong to a single organism. There will also be fresh grounds for realist belief.

Inclusive phenomenality

Because light and sound waves can be converted to information, stored and reproduced by machines, it is tempting to associate this process with biological vision and hearing. In the cases of taste and smell, it is less plausible that sensory inputs should be converted to information. I can watch a football match on TV or listen to music on the radio, but how could I experience a meal at a Michelin-starred restaurant without enjoying the thing itself? If an informational representation of a sensory experience is hard to imagine, it is also hard to imagine how the experience could be had non-consciously. We have no difficulty in accepting that a robot can register light or sound waves as information, but if it were required to process tastes and smells, it would likely be designed to analyze them chemically. Why should taste and smell involve afferent neurology, as they do in animals, unless they have become part of conscious experience?

If we granted phenomenal consciousness to other animals, however, we would massively extend the domain in which adequate explanation was lacking, for example of how conscious experiences could affect the body. Taking a human case, I might wake up one morning and look at the time: eight o'clock, which means that I cannot catch my flight to Rome. I immediately experience a sinking feeling in the stomach, together with an emotional rush. How could my conscious awareness of the time bring about these physical reactions? To be precise, how could conscious construal feed back to the physical brain? We can perhaps take it for granted that the brain is capable of stimulating physically expressed emotional responses. Other animals have the same ability to translate perceptual experience (sentient or otherwise) into a hormonal response, for example when secreting adrenaline.

The problem is associated with causation: there is no satisfactory explanation of the causal power of a mental state in respect of a brain state. But S-theory dispenses with causation. Instead conscious mental states non-causally necessitate brain states. The burden of explanation falls on this metaphysical relation, which is the essential subject of this investigation. If it can be explained, we can hypothesize a brain state corresponding to, for example, the perceptual experience of a predator or of a watch that says eight o'clock. The brain can use this 'information', held in some way at a physical level, to trigger emotional or behavioural responses with adaptive value. In that case we come back to a question raised earlier: why is the conscious experience necessary? In our case, it enables us to understand why we are experiencing an emotional reaction and therefore consciously to alter our behaviour. Next time I have a flight to catch, I will adapt by setting my alarm clock. In the case of an animal, evolutionary selection will have associated the brain state underlying the perceptual experience of a predator with an escape behaviour. The connection may have proved more reliable when the brain state has been modified by the kind of informed discrimination only sentience can provide. Imagine two species of animal, only one of which is sentient. Each animal 'sees' a leopard nearby. The non-sentient animal recognizes danger and takes evading action: a brain state has been associated by evolution with a physical response. The sentient animal, however, is able to synthesize visual information in a more sophisticated way. Its perceptual experience of the leopard is also based in a brain state, but a more complex one than the relevant brain state in the non-sentient animal. Let's assume that it incorporates the distance and speed of the leopard. The distinctive composition of this brain state has enabled evolution to associate it with a differentiated type of evading behaviour, one that suits the occasion more precisely than the evading behaviour of the non-sentient animal. Consequently, only the sentient animal outwits the leopard. In this indirect way sentience, and perceptual accuracy, may have been selected for. I would stress, however, that no extension of sentience is required by the theory that all brains have an afferent condition of satisfaction.

Perception as function

Perception can mean two slightly different things. It can denote a biological process involving neurophysiology and phenomenal experience or it can carry in addition an epistemological sense, in which case it implies that the subject's experience corresponds to something in the external world and is thereby to be distinguished from, for example, dreaming. Philosophers are more interested in the latter understanding of perception since they are concerned to establish, among other things, how we can have knowledge as distinct from mere belief, including knowledge about the external world. Unless a perceptual experience can be brought into relation with the object supporting it, we can no have means of anchoring perception outside our bodies. This would give rise to the possibility that perceptual experience, for all we know, might be illusory and have no bearing on the external world – that it might be a kind of dream. One reason why philosophers in general frown on internalism is that they take it to sever all ties between mind and world and therefore to jeopardize all knowledge except a person's awareness of his own thoughts and sensations.

Externalism, however, has been unable to theorize the ties between mind and world convincingly. In particular it is faced with the problem of circularity: to look for a relation of correspondence or appropriateness between an external object and its percept is to assume that there is an external object with properties appropriate to those of the percept. But because these sets of properties cannot be distinguished, appropriateness cannot be given meaning. If the contents of conscious experience had specific neural correlates and sensory stimuli produced invariant neurological states, the position would be different. We would be able to compare a subject's reported experience with his brain states and his brain states with the objects in his visual field. If his brain states confirmed his reported perception of a red car, but there was no red car in his visual field, we would need to revise our assumptions about the neurological patterns associated with red cars in the visual field. This would involve standard scientific procedure. However, as Freeman has led the way in pointing out, there is a lack of consistency in neural states: identical stimuli can produce different states on different occasions in the same animal subject. At the same time there is the previously discussed problem of the neural correlates of consciousness. Neurological states are not exposed to direct evolutionary pressure and therefore cannot be expected to settle into predictable patterns vis-à-vis phenomenal experience. Separating perceptual experience from the external object of perception, therefore, is a neurological stage that resists correlation in both directions. This schema is consistent with direct perception since the neurological stage need not be representational.

There is a further problem: sexually reproduced organisms are all different. Even if perchance the states of an individual brain could be predicted from visual stimuli or reported experience, there would be no reason to expect neural conformity between brains under identical stimuli and still less on identical reports. For good measure one might add the varying effects of hormones from brain to brain. So the kind of lawlike generalization familiar in physics, and applicable to computers or 'intelligent' machines, is absent from biology except at the microscopic levels where physical or chemical reactions can be controlled. Unlike a physical law, a lawlike generalization about a single organism is not of great interest. Biologists instead make a special kind of generalization across organisms in order to explain common function – how it came to exist, how it works and how it is served. Functional explanation, of which genome mapping is an example, has no counterpart in physics but is not for that reason inferior or less rigorous. The S-theorist will take a functional view of perception, rather as a biologist might take a functional view of digestion. In both digestion and perception the incorporation of generic inputs can have broadly predictable effects, while malfunction can be explained. But a biologist would not attempt to predict a physiological state from an ingested item of food.

Function emerges at higher levels of organization and is often visible to the naked eye; at lower levels biological processes may be lawlike. A discipline such as biochemistry confines itself to such processes. Cognitive neuroscience by contrast is concerned with both brain function (cognition) and the microscopic processes that support it. A researcher observing neuronal activity would find it difficult to banish functional considerations, such as the kind of psychological state with which the activity is associated. As a biologist, his impulse will be to link activity and function; as a scientist, he will look by default for lawlike correlation. However, psychological states do not correlate empirically. What happens next may be peculiar to cognitive neuroscience. In order to proceed, and with an eye to his colleagues in AI, the researcher adopts a *theoretical* commitment to correlation, perhaps assuming that it will be confirmed when our knowledge is more complete. Unfortunately this position is unfalsifiable – it could never be demonstrated that correlation is absent (we could never know that our knowledge was complete). On a Popperian view, the only genuine science is based on the testing of falsifiable hypotheses. At least that is how science is generally thought to advance.

It might be thought that philosophy would rise above such matters or find a solution; in fact it is also hostage to the dominant explanatory model, namely that of physics, while seeking to make sense of a rarified type of function, namely that of the mind. Owing to a certain physical view of matter, which appears to be the only one available, philosophy has been unable to escape the Cartesian straightjacket or to resist the reduction of biological to computational processes. It has never come to terms, on its own terms, with the distinctiveness of biological function; this would presuppose an appropriate metaphysics.

S has the merit of presaging such a metaphysics (its full implications will be considered in Chapter 3) and through it an alternative explanatory model. Its internalism undermines certainty about the external world but that is not in itself a reason for rejecting it; paradoxically it is less conducive to anti-realism than the dominant model. It can call on evolutionary theory to elucidate the organism's hermetic but dependable relation to the external world. In return it affords biology a new angle on the interrelation of organization, input, form and function. It offers a principled account of biological indeterminacy while indicating a deep coherence forged by historical events. In the following chapters I hope to show how it may ease certain other outstanding problems in philosophy.

CHAPTER 2

EXTENDING THE PHENOTYPE

Richard Dawkins's *The Extended Phenotype*, one of the most important contributions to evolutionary theory, advanced the idea that many animals are not limited by their physiological phenotypes but deploy or construct external objects as tools or other means of manipulating their environments in their favour. Examples are nests, sticks used for obtaining otherwise inaccessible food, stones on which the casings of edible objects are broken open, as well as spectacular achievements like the beaver's dam and the spider's web. Such objects can be described as *phenotypic extensions* because the relationship between animal and object is evolutionary. The object has become functional, like a neck or a heart, enhancing the animal's ability to survive and reproduce. Its skilled use will have been consolidated as instinct. The phenotypic extension may even be another animal, such as the bird that performs the service of hatching the cuckoo's egg.

Like the physiological phenotypic character, the phenotypic extension is a satisfaciend with its own conditions of satisfaction, namely the use or purpose to which the object is teleologically oriented. The spider's web does not cause flies to be trapped: that also requires that they fly into it. It is a contributory cause; it means the trapping of flies. The trapping of flies is the reason for the spider's web; the web is necessitated by fly-trapping. The web's meaning is realized when a fly is caught. When an animal uses a found object, such as a stick or a stone, to perform a task, the object becomes necessitated by the use to which it is put and acquires meaning.

I have found only passing references to the idea of a human extended phenotype. This may be because it is considered to add nothing to our knowledge. I hope to make a contrary case. Everything we make in order to use, from keys, watches and clothes to computers, cars and ships, can be classed as phenotypic extensions. We also use found objects as extensions, normally with some kind of modification. Unlike other animals, we can value our extensions, transfer them and buy them ready-made. We may discover extensions that we did not know existed but whose usefulness we immediately grasp. For these reasons the concept of the phenotypic extension may be thought to have weak applicability to humans. At first sight I do not appear to have an evolutionary relationship with my mobile phone. In fact we have gained leverage from what is essentially an evolutionary relation, conjuring our extended phenotype at will.

Like a bird's nest, many human extensions are shareable, notably dwellings and means of transport. When a human extension is shared, a certain type of relationship is created between the object's users, in which mutual expectation gives rise to obligation. The value of the object to each user is affected by the way the other users treat it, as each of them is aware. The maintenance of the object in a functional state is therefore a shared responsibility with a normative focus. If each user's relationship to the object were considered in isolation, this normative element would not be captured and his behaviour would not be fully explained. Individuals also form associations which create collective phenotypic extensions – objects that could not serve the same purpose for a solitary individual. Public buildings are perhaps the best example.

Phenotypic extensions, whether created by humans or other animals, serve a purpose; when we recognize a phenotypic extension, we grasp its expressed meaning; its realized meaning is its condition of satisfaction. An animal phenotypic extension will invariably have a physical connection to its condition of satisfaction: the spider's web will detain the fly, the beaver's dam the stream. The animal's instinctive manipulation of the extension will have been moulded by the physics of each situation, as would the evolution of a phenotypic character such as a tooth or a claw.

Humans, on the other hand, can first conceive of a desirable state of affairs and then create the means of achieving it. Consequently the S-axis from satisfaciend to condition of satisfaction may be epistemological in origin. Even so, the processes involved in the use of a mobile phone are all physical processes that have a claim to be real, since otherwise they would not fit together.

This duality can be seen most clearly in the case of *assigned* function. By affixing a small rectangle of sticky paper with limited causal powers, Mrs Trellis of North Wales is able to galvanize an industry into conveying her letter in less than 24 hours to the door of her friend 250 miles away. How is this possible? Whereas the functions of both phenotypic characters and extensions like cups and chairs are defined by their physical properties, human beings have discovered the benefits of imposing function on objects by collective fiat. An early example was the prize. An object was needed which had little or no intrinsic value but could be awarded in recognition of some achievement and continue as a public reminder. A desirable condition of satisfaction was conceived and a suitable satisfaciend invented. Similarly the postage stamp can serve no physical purpose but can have an imposed condition of satisfaction in the prompt delivery of a piece of mail to a specific destination. The fact that its condition of satisfaction involves a cost is represented by the price attached to this intrinsically worthless object. When the stamp was invented, a system was created that would govern how the condition of satisfaction would be realized. By invoking the assigned function in the prescribed way, an individual could independently achieve the desired result.

Mrs Trellis bought the stamp with money, perhaps the paradigm of assigned function. It illustrates how an assigned function can itself be assigned. Money first took the form of metals that had to be tested and weighed to arrive at a value – the value of the metal itself. To simplify matters, coins were invented. At first they were intended to be worth the value of the metal they contained but it was later realized that this strict association was unnecessary provided the issuing authority was credible. Indeed, being made of a worthless material solved the problem of clipping. Coins were thus assigned the function of carrying a specific exchangeable value, their condition of satisfaction being the fact of being exchanged for goods of similar value. This assigned function was subsequently reassigned to pieces of paper, which still in some cases carry a promise to pay the bearer on demand, that is, to reverse the assigned function. The banknote's *de facto* condition of satisfaction, however, is the fact of being exchanged for goods.

Ephemerality and directionality

A phenotypic extension can be *ephemeral*, for example when it is a vocalization. A textbook case is provided by vervet monkeys, who use a system of signals considered sophisticated even among primates. They have three separate alarm calls referring to eagles, snakes and leopards (or similar); each call prompts a different type of evading behaviour. There is debate over whether the calls are instinctive or learned, since young vervets sometimes make mistakes when calling. It appears that the inherited basis of alarm calls is causally insufficient to produce infallibility and requires reinforcement in the form of imitation, correction and practice.

Because our primary use of language is indicative or declarative, it is natural to assume that with its leopard alarm the vervet is trying to convey the equivalent of 'There is a leopard nearby.' One might imagine its fellow vervets processing this information against an internal rule of the form 'If a leopard is nearby, quickly climb the nearest tree.' In fact their behaviour would be no different if the alarm-raiser were trying to convey the equivalent of 'Take leopard-avoiding action!' or even 'Quickly climb the nearest tree!'

Except for internal organs, most physiological phenotypic characters operate on the external environment. Sense organs and sensory systems are unusual in being operated on by the external environment. In this sense phenotypic functions can be said to have *directionality*. I'll adopt the jargon of socketry and term outward directionality *male* and inward *female*. If the body itself is considered as an environment, internal organs like hearts and lungs can be said to have male directionality. Phenotypic extensions also exhibit directionality. The beaver's dam and the spider's web, although fixed, operate on the animal's environment, in a way comparable to most human inventions. However, some human extensions have female directionality. These include maps, signposts, clocks, sundials, barometers, speedometers and any device that measures or records images, sounds or temperatures. Modes of transport can be classed as male, since they bring about changes in passengers' relationships to the world. Dwellings and other forms of protection are not directionally female but neither are they obviously male. We should allow for the possibility that extensions be non-directional; human examples might be furniture and clothes.

It appears that the phenotypic extensions of other animals invariably have either male or no directionality: there is no animal equivalent of a map or a clock. The same is true of their ephemeral extensions. The conditions of satisfaction of animal signals are behaviours on the part of other animals of the same species. Animals vocalize for a variety of reasons, so we should distinguish signals by defining them as necessitated by advantageous behaviours on the part of individuals other than the signaller. When one animal causes another to leave its territory by means of vocalization, the departure does not necessitate the warning – it could be prompted by visual input. Similarly a vocalization that forms part of a mating ritual is not necessitated by the outcome unless it is the only clue offered by the vocalizer, in which unlikely case it can be treated as a signal. As with the gene, selection operates on the signal's condition of satisfaction: vervets survive partly because they are better at avoiding danger than other species. Because the cost to the signaller, in terms of energy or risk, is on balance outweighed by the benefit to other vervets of the signal, a reciprocal system has been able to evolve.

The parsing instinct is common to any animal capable of recognizing a new instance of a familiar type, be it a type of predator, a type of food, a member of its own species or an object suitable for use as a phenotypic extension. Recognition is evolutionarily linked to advantageous behaviour. The evolutionary association of a parsed instance with a specific signal means that advantageous behaviour can be linked in individuals other than the signaller to recognition of the signal. As a behavioural response the signal is only remarkable because it does not directly benefit the signaller.

The condition of satisfaction of a physical phenotypic extension with male directionality is some external physical effect, such as the trapping of a fly or the turning of a screw. But what about the female extension? One might be tempted to identify its condition of satisfaction with its purpose; if the purpose of a sundial is to measure time, surely this is its condition of satisfaction. But what kind of thing is the measurement of time? If it is a condition of satisfaction, it must in some sense exist over and above the existence of time itself. But in what domain could it exist? Suppose that someone who had no knowledge of sundials came across one on a sunny day and was looking at it, perhaps trying to work out what it was. Would there be any measurement of time? If no one were looking at any of the sundials or timepieces that exist, would there be any measurement? These objects consist of materials whose behaviour is predictable enough to support measurement but it cannot be found *in* those materials or in the way they are manipulated. The sundial has no moving parts and so does not do anything. This is a different question from any concerning the existence of the sundial when not being perceived. While the mind-independent existence of the sundial may be the best explanation of our experience of it, there is nothing that the mind-independent measurement of time is the best explanation of.

I suggest that the sundial's condition of satisfaction is a cognitive state, namely the state of awareness in an informed observer of the time of day. The speedometer's condition of satisfaction is the driver's state of awareness of the speed of her vehicle. In these cases incorporands take the form of the psychological resources required to 'read' the female extension.

This means that we do not need to explain the relationship between the mind and the measurement: they coincide. We naturally project or externalize the conditions of satisfaction of female extensions because their cognitive effects are transparent to us. If they were not transparent, they would be a pointless encumbrance. Consequently even philosophers who have reflected deeply on the matter may consider female extensions to be objectively representational. A similar displacement beneficially affects perception: because our perceptual experience occurs transparently, we can project perceptual effects and identify them with external objects.

The origin of the female extension may resemble that of an assigned function. We conceive a particular state of awareness as advantageous, such as knowing the time of day or the speed of the car we're driving, and then invent an appropriate satisfaciend. When the female extension is defined as having a cognitive condition of satisfaction rather than as reflecting external conditions, other objects are seen to qualify, including books, radios and musical instruments. It would not be surprising if the ability to entertain cognitive, in addition to perceptual, conditions of satisfaction required a highly evolved brain, perhaps of larger than average size. (There is no scientific basis for the myth that the human brain is partly unused.) My guess is that, for obvious reasons, a biped would be more likely than a quadruped to achieve the cognitive breakthrough.

The male extension can now be redefined as that which is not female; non-directionality can be discarded as a category. While male extensions have observable physical effects, the female extension is more complex. We construe the object's expressed meaning, as we would that of a male extension, but we also entertain its condition of satisfaction in realized meaning as a necessitating cognitive state. When the female extension is permanent, these effects can often be distinguished: we can recognize a sundial on a dull day or a speedometer in a stationary car without entertaining their conditions of satisfaction. But what might it be like if the female extension were ephemeral?

Before turning to this question, I should address an important point, which may not have escaped you. If the sundial is a satisfaciend with cognitive conditions of satisfaction, the principle that an external object only acquires psychological presence through the mechanisms of binding and parsing will be flouted. Just as an external object cannot necessitate a psychological state, there could conversely be no necessitation of the sundial itself by a state of awareness of the time of day. In fact it is not the sundial but its percept that functions as satisfaciend. This is possible because to the conscious subject there is no distinction between the external and the perceived sundial. The cognitive S-axis, like the perceptual, is thus confined to the subject's physiology.

Semantic meaning

I believe that human language evolved from signalling. I do not pretend that this is an original insight, neither do I intend to make an argument, since nothing could count strongly enough as evidence. Instead I hope to show that the hypothesis can illuminate and help make sense of the way language works. In a nutshell, I suggest that the behavioural condition of satisfaction became a cognitive condition of satisfaction by virtue of the signal's cognitive transit. In other words, at some point one of our ancestors heard an alarm signal and consciously recognized its significance. In addition to its perceptual meaning, the signal acquired meaning in the consciousness of the hearer, not merely in his behaviour. Its cognitive meaning identified the cause of the alarm instead of merely prescribing its effect. The vocalization continued as a satisfaciend but switched to female directionality as a language item. It became *semantic*; the signaller effectively became a namer.

Although the name can be regarded as the original and fundamental semantic unit, it has been superseded in this role by the *sentence*. A speaker can use a sentence to prompt in a hearer a state of awareness about a state of affairs removed from the hearer's purview either in time or space. If a speaker merely says

'Snake!', his audience cannot infer anything more than a warning of immediate danger. Specifying whether the snake is large or small, nearby or distant, dangerous or innocuous, stationary or moving, requires a *contingent* sentence, in which an entity is picked out by a name and described with the aid of other parts of speech. The hearer's own perceptual field is thereby extended; his state of awareness necessitates the speaker's sentence. Once sentences are seen to have this power, they can be used by a language-sharing group to assemble a repository of knowledge about their world, to which individuals can contribute while at the same time being able to extract adaptive value. The repository becomes an evolutionary asset, mediating selection pressures at the individual level. The human brain increases in size over a remarkably short period, linked to the development of language and the formation of shareable knowledge. Humans become uniquely social beings with an environment consisting of the known universe. With the invention of writing, knowledge can be objectified, systematized and accumulated.

Language will have reached maturity before the invention of writing. When declarative sentences were first constructed, they would normally have been meant, that is, used intentionally to bring about states of awareness ('There is a snake behind you'). While I can put in front of you the sentence 'The fourth bear is wearing Austrian morning dress', and you will understand it, I may not mean it. That is, I may have no intention of making you aware of a state of affairs; it could just be an invented sentence. Unmeant sentences are actually quite rare outside philosophy, linguistics and language learning. When a declarative sentence is meant, it becomes a *statement*. Only as a statement does the sentence have a condition of satisfaction in another's state of awareness. Here the distinction between construed and realized meaning comes into play. When you understand the meaning of 'The fourth bear is wearing Austrian morning dress', you merely construe its *sense*. The realization of its meaning requires receptivity to the intention of the speaker or writer and is inseparable from a type of belief about the sentence's content. If this is improbable, the belief is less likely to be formed.

Sense is conditional on the sentence's being syntactically well-formed. If I say to you 'Emblem often Austrian morning dress clever mention', you will understand the individual words and you may think I am trying to assemble a sentence. But you will not be able to make sense of it. In attempting to do so, you will call on the same resources you use when constructing sentences, namely deeply ingrained assumptions about syntactic protocol as well as familiarity with compound expressions like 'morning dress'. The syntactic construction of sense is an example of novelty enabled by plasticity and has the characteristics of a *gestalt* process, that is, one in which the resulting whole is something more than the sum of its parts. Before the invention of writing, sentences would have been heard word by word; each word could prompt a re-evaluation of overall sense and modify the hearer's anticipation of the final meaning of the sentence.

A neat illustration of syntactic plasticity is the pet fish experiment. When people are asked to list pets, they will likely say 'dog, cat, budgie, hamster' etc. When asked to list fish, it might be 'cod, salmon, trout, shark' etc. When asked to list pet fish, people normally start with 'goldfish' or 'guppy'. The point at issue in linguistics is how psychologically this answer is arrived at. Do we have internal lists of pets and fish, which we run down until we come to a name common to both? Or is 'pet fish' semantically unitary and conceptually *gestalt*? We might say that goldfish and guppies are good examples of pet fish. If the expression were not a semantic fusion, the origin of this intuition would be a mystery since goldfish are not particularly good examples of pets or fish. Compound expressions like 'pet fish' do not become unitary through familiarity: we constantly invent and grasp new ones with little effort.

What then is the relation of word meaning to the meaning of complex expressions including sentences? If words had their own conditions of satisfaction, from which sentence meaning were somehow constructed by the hearer, the sentence itself could not form a satisfaciend. Like sentences, words have sense. But when do individual words have realized meaning? Only when they are used as imperatives, as replies to questions, as labels ('Exit', 'Ambulance'), as interrogatives ('How?', 'When?') or as conventional exclamations ('Shame!', 'Congratulations!'). I deal with imperatives in Chapter 3; suffice it to say at this point that they do not bring about the same kind of awareness as declarative sentences. A single-word reply to a question obviates its being restated as a sentence, just as an interrogative stands for a complete question. Similarly a label abbreviates a sentence of the form 'This is an X'. So it is safe to say that, apart from exclamations (to which I return briefly later in this chapter), individual words never compete with declarative sentences as satisfaciends.

Nevertheless it is unlikely that our ancestors began to use sentences as soon as the transition from signalling was made. The first step would have been the use of individual words by speakers intending to prompt states of awareness, for example the awareness of specific danger. Personal proper names may have emerged quite early as a means of identification and may have catalyzed the development of the sentence as a means of describing personal behaviour. It may be that to this end names were originally combined with descriptive gestures. This is all highly speculative; my tentative point is that the cognitive apparatus originally associated with realized word meaning may have survived the emergence of the sentence as part of the psychological mechanism activated in the hearer by a statement.

Sense and reference

Semantic meaning has been a preoccupation of Anglo-Saxon philosophers for over a century, although the seminal figure is often taken to be a German, Gottlob Frege. In a paper of (1892) he famously distinguished between *Sinn* and *Bedeutung*, normally translated as *sense* and *reference*. In fact J. S. Mill had made a similar distinction between *connotation* and *denotation* in (1843). Another similar distinction is made between *intension* and *extension*. Although sense, connotation and intension are subtly different, there is no mileage to be had in distinguishing between denotation, reference and extension. They all convey the notion that names correspond to bits of the world (*referents*), which may be single entities, substances or kinds. Stones, mountains and planets are examples of kinds.

A name's reference is commonly assumed to be part of its meaning since it is otherwise difficult to see how its sense could remain constant and grounded. For Frege the sense of a name contained the referent's mode of representation to the subject who understood it. This allows a single referent to have multiple names with different senses (and for the same name to have different senses for different people). Frege illustrated the point with the Morning Star and the Evening Star, names used in the past with different senses for what we know to be a single object (the planet Venus) and therefore a single referent. He was distancing himself from Mill, who took proper names to denote without connoting. Thus the town of Dartmouth is so called because it stands at the mouth of the River Dart. But the name does not *mean* that it stands there. If the river changed its course and the town was no longer at its mouth, there would be no reason to change its name. For Mill the name originally had a connotation, which had atrophied. One could accept this point but still believe that the name Dartmouth may have a sense for someone who recognizes it. It might, for example, carry a naval sense *for a particular hearer*. A Spaniard might be familiar with the name Dartmouth, perhaps because a friend had gone to live there, without being aware of the River Dart or the riverine sense of 'mouth'. For him the representational sense of the name Dartmouth would not be connotative.

A problem faced by Frege is that what appears to be a meaningful word or compound expression may lack a reference, examples being 'unicorn', 'phlogiston', 'the planet between Mercury and the Sun' and 'the present King of France'. He deplored the fact that ordinary language could contain such expressions and considered sentences constituted from them ('Unicorns have four legs and a tail', 'The present King of France is wise') to be deficient in meaning. They would be deficient if truth, as is widely held, were essential to meaning since their truth cannot be established: verification would depend on finding the referent. But a non-referring singular expression ('The first person to walk on Mars') can form part of a sentence ('The first person to walk on Mars will be famous') that is not only meaningful but apparently true, even though it may never be verified. I return later in this chapter to the relation of truth to meaning.

On S-theory as applied to semantic meaning, individual words only have sense or expressed meaning, except in the five special cases (imperatives, answers, interrogatives, labels and exclamations); realized meaning is the preserve of statements and can only be cognitive. Reference or referents form no part of the meaning of names or statements. These can both be said to refer, where reference is a description of their use. Take the vervet's leopard alarm. We could say that the signaller is referring to the leopard or that the signal refers to it, but the meaning of the signal is behavioural. Similarly, when a person uses the word 'mountain', he refers to a mountain or mountains. The construed meaning of what is going on contains reference to the mountain. But the mountain is not what is being meant. If you have difficulty in excising reference from meaning, imagine you are the first primate or hominid consciously to understand the meaning of an alarm signal, while your fellows still respond behaviourally. The alteration in your psychology is not referential: the connection between the signal and the danger already exists.

So the sentence 'Unicorns have four legs and a tail' lacks nothing in meaning, except insofar as a hearer, who knows that unicorns do not exist, will not allow sentences about them to prompt in him states of awareness that presuppose their existence. However, nothing prevents a person from forming a state of awareness about an imaginary creature and no mechanism appears to inhibit this kind of awareness. It may be significant that as children we master language before becoming expert at distinguishing the imaginary from the real. Culturally also, we have since the seventeenth century become more rigorous in distinguishing them, while using sentences in the traditional way.

Having excluded reference from meaning, the S-theorist has the task of explaining how sense alone can be stabilized. Because the explanation is evolutionary, it may well be unacceptable to analytic philosophers. But a satisfactory account of reference – how things connect with their names – has not been forthcoming from that quarter. Some hope is reposed in externalist semantics, especially by naturalizing philosophers. The idea is that, because minds as physical systems are part of the unitary causal economy of the closed physical universe, the functions of mental objects such as words are likely to be determined in a causal fashion by external conditions. Under a version of externalism presented by Hilary Putnam (1975), names of *natural kinds*, such as spiders and gold, exist as reflections of real distinctions between the microstructural properties of objects and substances. One of the tasks of science is to uncover these mind-independent properties. Natural kinds are scientifically robust: experimental evidence based on a sample of a natural kind can be used to predict how all samples of the same kind will behave. If the prediction fails, a new natural kind will have been identified and will need a name. The adoption and use of natural kind names in natural language is expected to have the same kind of causal explanation as any other natural phenomenon.

Natural kinds owe something to real distinctions but it is clear that we have a practical, pragmatic relationship with them. In the early nineteenth century, mineralogists discovered that the term 'jade' had been applied indiscriminately to what they now decided were two different minerals, to be called *jadeite* and *nephrite*. This distinction still shows no sign of catching on; the difference in the minerals' microstructure may never be sufficient to affect us. Conversely, in the case of the many Inuit words for types of snow, which are not synonyms, kinds have proliferated beyond any scientific rationale, for what are clearly adaptational reasons. A word like 'mountain' behaves like a natural kind name, but mountains are not natural kinds since nothing ontologically distinguishes them from hills. 'Unicorn' and 'phlogiston' behave just like natural kind names although no one would suggest they are natural kinds. If you believe that the meanings of words are determined by facts about the world, you have to explain how words can have been meant before the relevant facts were understood, for example how the word 'water' can have been meant before the chemical composition of water was discovered.

A related project to Putnam's was that of Saul Kripke (1972), who coined the term 'rigid designation' to describe the referring behaviour of names. Rather like Mill, he found it difficult to attribute sense to proper names since this would seem to make them equivalent to definite descriptions, a view associated with Bertrand Russell. If a name, such as Aristotle, means (has the sense of) 'the teacher of Alexander', 'the inventor of biology' or 'the greatest philosopher', a sentence such as 'Aristotle was the greatest philosopher' should be no more meaningful than 'The greatest philosopher was the greatest philosopher'. But it clearly is more meaningful. According to Kripke, it could have happened that someone other than Aristotle was the teacher of Alexander, but it could not have happened that someone other than Aristotle – that particular individual, rigidly designated – was Aristotle. So the name functions in a different way from any description.

There is a sense in which names, including common names, rigidly designate. 'Gold' carries the sense of a yellowish, malleable metal. But suppose that a cosmic event caused all gold to become blue and brittle. We would probably carry on calling it 'gold': the word would change its representational sense while continuing to refer to the same substance. But it does not follow that its persistent reference would be part of its meaning.

To see the problem for Kripke's position, take the sentence 'Some scholars believe that Shakespeare was the Earl of Oxford'. These scholars do not believe that the person born in Stratford-on-Avon and married to Anne Hathaway was the Earl of Oxford; they believe that the plays attributed to him were written by the Earl of Oxford. So the name 'Shakespeare', to someone understanding the sentence to have that import, which it can clearly bear, does not rigidly designate Kripke-fashion. Instead it has a kind of transferable representational sense. A further problem is that a person of sound mind may be unaware that two familiar names refer to the same individual. A favourite example is Lois Lane, who knows Clark Kent and knows of Superman, but has only come to suspect that they are the same person. Something similar can occur with common names. A person might sound off confidently about the culinary virtues of coriander and cilantro without realizing they are the same plant. The referentialist has to explain how this is possible, if the words mean (in the referentialist's sense) the same plant.

Kripke went on to address the question of how a proper name becomes attached to its referent. He suggested that an initial act of 'dubbing' takes place, for example when a baby is given a name. The association of person and name then follows through causal interaction between speakers and hearers, in which the referent somehow figures. The same kind of associative process must attach names to fictional characters. Kripke did not commit himself to a causal theory of reference, aware perhaps how farfetched it is. But it has no serious competitor as a theory of referential meaning, which may be why its inherent circularity is tolerated. The naming activity of a speaker would have to have a causal effect firstly on a hearer's construed perception, but the requirement that the naming activity be independent of its perception cannot be met. Similarly the natural kind is construed in perception and therefore cannot be party to a non-circular causal relation with any perceptual state. In pre-scientific cultures the microstructural properties of natural kinds cannot even be construed. A causal theory of reference is even less plausible than a causal theory of perception since the perception of the naming activity or the natural kind would additionally have to cause a psychological disposition to use a name correctly and to continue to do so.

The key to an S-based theory of semantic meaning is a distinction between parsing and naming, in which parsing is evolutionarily and therefore psychologically prior, while naming is essentially a form of associated behaviour, like signalling. The attachment of the name to the parsed object or substance is thus the legacy of an adaptation, forged under selective pressure and strongly contributing to the stabilization of sense. Because we have the capacity to invent phenotypic extensions, we can invent new names. Because they are ephemeral, they exhibit something of the flexibility of assigned function. However, they are normally derived or copied, which gives them a ready-made representational sense.

Externalist philosophers tend to sympathize with cognitive scientists over the difficulty they face in explaining how, on their assumptions, naming is possible. In computational terms a name is a symbol with no intrinsic semantic content but only a repeatable form; it has only a contingent relation to what it denotes. In cognitive science, therefore, the *symbol-grounding problem* looms large: how can an empty symbol become reliably attached to what it denotes *within* the syntactic system of which it is a part and without the aid of an external imposer or realizer of meaning? This is essentially the issue highlighted by Searle with his Chinese Room. An externalist or naturalizing philosopher is likely to reject Searle's point and to assume that the problem of semantic meaning *is* the symbol-grounding problem. Both will therefore be solved simultaneously. In fact the solving of the former with reference to biology may reveal the latter to be a problem only for artificial intelligence and therefore of limited interest. Names are not arbitrary symbols, nor do they require grounding in external reality. They are behavioural phenomena with a non-contingent relation to discriminatory states of awareness.

Linguistic intension

It would be a mistake to assume that parsing is based exclusively on a passive processing of visual stimuli or, to put in another way, that the neurology of parsing is purely afferent. I occasionally imagine being in the shoes of Rick Deckard, the hero of Ridley Scott's *Blade Runner*, whose job description involves tracking down and identifying the dangerous, life-like androids or 'replicants' who have made their way from the off-world colony where they were kept as slaves. They can be distinguished either by a laborious and not very cinematographic testing of their bone marrow or by means of interrogation, at which Deckard excels. He asks his suspects questions that would evoke an emotional response in a human being and then measures it.

Are there any alternative strategies? I would try showing the subject three pictures of ordinary dining chairs: one with some small sharp spikes protruding downwards from the seat, one with spikes protruding upwards from the seat and one with spikes protruding from behind the back. I would casually ask what these three objects were. No unprepared human being would unhesitatingly and unequivocally call the second a chair. A phenotypic extension is defined primarily by its conditions of satisfaction, which in the case of the second object cannot exist. Nevertheless a form of natural kind parsing is also at work: given the need for complete coverage, the second object cannot be allowed to fall through the net unnamed: a human being would not unequivocally deny that it was a chair. The conflict provoked presents itself in consciousness as indecision. An android would experience the same conflict only if it had been designed with a feel for phenotypic extensibility. On any conceivable AI model, this could only be cosmetic.

Word use is comparable with the exercise of the phenotype in motor behaviour. When a young animal plays, it practises the use of its limbs and senses. With time its use becomes expert and its movements appear to be carefully judged. But, as we saw in Chapter 1, the expertise is a function of efferent neurology worked by practice into channels that support unconsciously directed behaviour. Tom Mitchell, Marcel Just and colleagues (2008) have found that the same area of motor cortex is engaged when an object is deployed as when the word denoting the object is recognized. For example, a subject asked to think about a hammer will show a response localized to the area of the brain active when he uses a hammer. When an infant learns how to use a word, his pre-conscious efferent neurology is trained as if he were learning how to deploy a limb, except that feedback takes the form of others' responses. The child becomes aware of the power of words to elicit reactions. He gradually acquires a vocabulary and uses it to construct original sentences. He is evolutionarily disposed to learn to use language, just as he is equipped to master efficient limb use. Feedback enables the child to coordinate his usage with his intention, but when the relevant neurological pathway has been set, he need rely less on feedback for accuracy. Words emerge pre-consciously. We hear ourselves utter them. Only then can we judge whether our choice has been appropriate, unless we have rehearsed what we intend to say. Just as we feel conscious control over our limbs, we feel control over our words because their intention-appropriateness has become reliable through practice.

Language therefore differs from most permanent female extensions in being purposefully wielded. In this respect it retains a vestige of the maleness of the signal: we use it to manipulate the psychology of hearers. A wielded language item will always bear the stamp of a speaker's purpose and will have efferent characteristics. Because the channels for word use and understanding double up, what we tellingly refer to as our *grasp* of linguistic meaning will also betray efference. A distinction between sense and *intension* is therefore in order. Intension can be used to denote the *activity* of meaning or understanding by a speaker or hearer, while sense abstracts the capacity to mean of a word or sentence. Intension will always be native to an individual language user: a word used by one person can never be guaranteed to have the same intension when used by another. Who, after all, would be the judge except a third person with his own intensional bias?

Word use is not surprisingly a focus of normativity. But compare the normativity associated with a shared phenotypic extension, such as a house, whose purpose is settled by its physical form. The normativity of word use derives less from purpose than from convergence, which can shift purpose. Pedantic as I am, I used to be irritated by hearing the word 'decimate' employed without the sense 'reduce by one tenth' until someone pointed out that its original meaning is not particularly useful, now that legions are no longer decimated. The word survives thanks to its new sense of 'reduce drastically', which I am willing to adopt. My residual reluctance is not due to some etymological normativity. It is my willingness to shift that is due to normativity: there is a party I risk missing. My guess is that this normativity is rooted in the evolutionary pressure to produce the most effective signal in a given circumstance. This, I suggest, is the basis of the stability of word sense. This bias to convergence will always take advantage of the available instruments: one of the Foucauldian by-products of scientific culture has been greater enforceability of semantic and orthographic convergence. It is no coincidence that the dictionary acquired its modern form at the cultural tipping-point towards the scientific worldview.

There is a barrier to convergence when words denote sensations, especially when these are not accompanied by customary behaviour. When we want to differentiate pains, for example, we tend to rely on imagery such as piercing and throbbing. We can estimate another person's pain level by assessing their behaviour. But some sensations are quite private. I have a problem with the concept of vertigo in that I do not know whether or not I suffer from it. It is of no use my looking the word up in a dictionary, where it is defined as a type of giddiness or dizziness caused by looking down from a great height. This is surely common to everyone in certain circumstances. Then again, I am unsure whether giddiness or dizziness accurately describes my sensation. Vertigo might manifest itself differently in different people. I do not know how to use the word precisely or to rectify the situation, since I do not entirely trust other people to know what vertigo is either.

Wittgenstein believed that we learn how to use words in a social context where what they denote can be pointed to. In this way usage is standardized. A question that therefore interested him was how one could be sure one was using a name consistently when one used it to describe a private sensation such as a pain. Suppose one had a small repertoire of private sensations to which one wanted to give names. Suppose further that these names were to be specially invented and not written down. How could one be certain that one was using each name 'correctly', when one had no support from the evidence of other people's usage or from their reactions to one's own usage?

This is an example of a philosophical problem to which scientific findings are relevant. Language is a social activity, as Wittgenstein stressed: the conditions of satisfaction of statements are states of awareness in others. There can be no feedback when language is private. Nevertheless, when word use is practised, neurological pathways are formed: something real happens that contributes to the accuracy of future usage. The question is whether word use could be practised without feedback. Social feedback in respect of word use resembles sensorimotor feedback in respect of motor behaviour, except that new words appear all the time: somebody must be inventing them. If I were to set myself the task of using an invented private name consistently, I would need first to associate it with a sensation (I could call my vertiginous sensation 'woowoosh') and then immediately start practising it. My feeling is that it would quite quickly stick. I could never be certain that my use was consistent, but neither can I be certain that when I use the word 'mountain' it is going to mean to other people what I expect it to mean or whether I am using it in the same way I last used it.

Facts and propositions

The primary use of language is the wielding of declarative sentences as statements, by speakers who mean them, that is, who aim to bring about specific states of awareness in hearers. Not all states of awareness necessitate statements. A speaker is unlikely to inform a hearer of a state of affairs that the hearer can perceive for himself unless the speaker wishes to reinforce the perception ('This cat is very friendly'). When a sentence is used as a storage device, it may become detached from the intention of a particular speaker. For example, it might form part of an inscription recording a significant event. Those who subsequently read the inscription understand it as meant, even though they cannot know who meant it and cannot imagine that the author had them in mind. Even in oral traditions before writing, the capacity of sentences to mean will have been lifted out of the directly personal context in which language emerged. When directly addressed, the individual will maintain a critical stance towards the information he is receiving with a view to synthesizing it with what he already knows or believes. When communication is depersonalized, we would expect there to be some kind of externalization of the critical stance. Since the information network inherits the individual's bias to coherence, it will tend to enforce conformity to public norms governing the quality of the information permitted to enter the repository. These norms constitute the mechanism by means of which the adaptive functionality of the repository is maintained. Under certain conditions the intrinsic conservatism of the repository may be overcome by a compelling new interpretation of available evidence. This may even set in train a deep revision of the basis of knowledge, as has been happening since the seventeenth century. The main instrument of epistemic normativity is the concept of truth.

Just as words appear to refer to objects, sentences appear to refer to states of affairs. A relationship of some kind appears to exist between a well-formed declarative sentence and a certain condition of the world. The nature of this relationship is even more problematic than the relationship of name to object since the state of affairs may be quite complex and abstract, as in 'Jenny studied mathematics at Cambridge.' This makes it implausible that the meaning of such a sentence should be causally related to a set of physical events. Instead, sentence meaning is normally investigated with reference to truth. What would make a sentence true appears to coincide with what it means. The state of affairs to which it refers is the conditions under which the sentence would be true. To grasp the meaning of 'Jenny studied mathematics at Cambridge' is to apprehend its *truth conditions*.

But look at the following sentences:

(1) Jenny is in Copenhagen.
(2) My sister is in Copenhagen.
(3) I am in Copenhagen.

(2) is uttered by Jenny's brother and (3) by Jenny herself. That is, all three sentences are about the same person and indicate that that person is in Copenhagen. If the same state of affairs is reflected by the different sentences, then the referential meanings of the three sentences must somehow coincide. This is explained on the hypothesis that the sentences express the same *proposition*. It is an aspect of language use that Jenny does not say 'Jenny is in Copenhagen', but she means the same thing as the person who uses this sentence of her; this thing is a proposition. It is immediately clear that the proposition would be a more reliable bearer of truth than the sentence. It distills the underlying meaning of the sentence, whose form is dependent on the circumstances of speakers, and clarifies its relation to the language-independent state of affairs. It is propositions therefore rather than sentences or statements that are generally held to have truth conditions. A sentence partakes of the meaning of the proposition it expresses. It can be translated into another language – become a different sentence – and still express the same proposition.

A true proposition is often considered to state, to correspond to or even to be a *fact*. If Jenny is in Copenhagen, it is a fact that Jenny is in Copenhagen. When Jenny's brother says his sister is in Copenhagen, he is articulating the same fact. Facts are useful because they can be used to make inferences. If Jenny is in Copenhagen, it is also a fact that she is not in London. Do these facts exist? In what kind of domain could they exist? Is there any limit to the number of facts? In the fact we are clearly dealing with a metaphysical entity; the proposition that Jenny is in Copenhagen is also a metaphysical entity. If two metaphysical entities are flagged by the same sentence, it is difficult to see how they could be distinguished.

Now consider the sentence 'Tomorrow is Thursday.' If propositions exist, there is no reason to doubt that one lurks here. The problem is that its truth conditions vary. On a Wednesday the proposition is true, but on every other day false. Although the expressed meaning of the sentence is unambiguous, it has to be treated as a context-specific statement if the underlying proposition is to emerge unambiguously. Similarly, for sentences (1) and (2) above to contain the same proposition, (2) must be a statement by Jenny's brother. It must also be uttered at the same time as (1); otherwise it might be false while (1) is true, making it a different proposition. Notice that the specific meaning attributed to the proposition cannot be recovered from a mere sentence: it requires a statement. But statements are riddled with intension.

Just as names may refer to non-existent entities, sentences may refer to non-existent states of affairs. If sentences such as 'Hamlet murdered Polonius' and 'Santa Claus lives above the Arctic Circle' contain propositions, their truth conditions cannot exist. But this has no impact on the sentences' meaning, which can be fully realized.

The case I want to make is that neither facts nor propositions exist. Rather they are externalizations of the cognitive conditions of satisfaction of statements. We externalize cognitive conditions of satisfaction for the same reason that we externalize perceptual conditions of satisfaction: they are transparent to us. Externalized, they become useful points of reference but cannot advance an analysis of natural language. Propositions belong to logic and mathematics: $2 + 3 = 5$ is a proposition but it is not the same proposition as $(6 - 4) + 3 = 5$. Because natural language is thought to be amenable to logical analysis, which is expected to help solve the problem of semantic meaning, philosophers in general have had no compunction about importing the concept of the proposition from logic. The notable exception was W. V. Quine (1970), who argued that propositions in natural language cannot be individuated because of the indeterminacy of the sense of sentences, and therefore do not exist.

The proposition reflects the fact that several individuals can entertain similar cognitive conditions of satisfaction, for example the awareness that a certain person is in Copenhagen, in response to different sentences. It is true therefore that the sentences have something in common but it is only to be found at the level of realized meaning, which will vary from person to person. If a satisfactory account of truth-conditional semantics, based on the proposition, were available, then we might be compelled to accept the existence of propositions. But, as Michael Dummett (2006) has pointed out, truth-conditional semantics are inherently circular. Understanding the meaning of a proposition involves apprehending its external correlates – its truth conditions. But these can only be apprehended in language; to be precise, the language in which the proposition is framed. A person who did not already understand the proposition would have no access to its truth conditions. Yet again circularity haunts an attempt to account for psychological function by appeal to externality.

Factual inference is a form of cognitive construal that can be represented in terms of the 'logical form' of propositions and the relations of entailment between them. But there is no more reason to think that the mind obeys this type of logic than that it devises chess moves like the computer programmed to beat it. The mind is far better at inference than any artificial imitator precisely because it does not rely solely on simple, overt facts. Unlike Cyc, it possesses a massive, finely tuned background awareness harnessed to adaptive construal without the benefit of propositional content. In logic a proposition is either true or false, but this cannot be said straightforwardly of many declarative sentences. Consider 'Cats are friendly', 'Gordon Brown is tall' and 'The population of London is 7.5 million.'

Although the 'logical form' of propositions is believed to make for clarity, it is a chimera responsible for wholly unnecessary complications. Because Superman and Clark Kent are the same person, the sentences 'Superman is very strong' and 'Clark Kent is very strong' are thought to harbour the same proposition. If Kripke was right about proper names, it should be possible to substitute 'Superman' for 'Clark Kent', and vice versa, in any proposition without altering its meaning. The conventional way of testing for an alteration in meaning is to look for a change in truth value (if two contingent propositions always have the same truth values, that is, neither is ever true when the other is false, then they are the same proposition). Since, with Kripke, the meaning of a proper name is its bearer, how the bearer is designated should make no difference to the proposition's truth value. Thus in sentences like 'Clark Kent lives at 678 Pacific Heights', 'Clark Kent' can be replaced with 'Superman' without a change in propositional meaning. But if, in the sentence 'Lois is looking for Clark', we substituted 'Superman' for 'Clark', there would be a change. At a certain moment, it could be true that Lois is looking for Clark but false that she is looking for Superman. *In a sense* she is looking for Superman but in a *primary* sense she is not.

This primary sense can be captured by designating the verb 'to look for' as an *intensional verb*. To say that Lois is looking for Clark but not for Superman is to preserve what would be Lois's first-person account of the matter and to respect her epistemic relation to the individual variously known as Clark and Superman. In other words the verb reflects Lois's own intensional stance. Other intensional verbs are 'to imagine', 'to expect' and 'to want'. A dehydrated person could want water without wanting H_2O, if he thought H_2O was a brand of rat poison. On the other hand he would need H_2O, even if he thought it was a brand of rat poison: 'to need' is not an intensional verb.

Although the intensional verb makes intension explicit, it is always present when the circumstances of an utterance are relevant to its sense. A case that exercised both Frege and Kripke concerns the Morning and Evening Stars. As their names suggest, at one time these were understandably thought to be distinct objects; we now know that they are both the planet Venus. As a proposition, 'The Morning Star is the Evening Star' is known as a statement of identity and is therefore in logic true necessarily – it could not be the case that the object in question be different from itself. But, as Kripke noticed, there must have been a point when a person, perhaps the discoverer of the identity, could have uttered the sentence in the sense 'What we think of as the Morning Star is also – surprise, surprise – the Evening Star'. He will thereby have prompted an epistemic reappraisal of the object and its mode of reference; he will have been *establishing* the identity in the minds of his audience. To treat his utterance as an identity statement would be to ignore the particularity of its conditions of satisfaction when made. In order to achieve his paradox, Kripke had to specify the context of the utterance and the speaker's communicative intent, thereby introducing intension.

Kripke believed that 'The Morning Star is the Evening Star' contains a necessary *a posteriori* proposition, that is, a proposition which, while unable to be false (the identity statement), had to be discovered empirically to be true. His interest was due to the fact that propositions had been assumed to be either necessary and *a priori* or contingent and *a posteriori*. The *a priori/a posteriori* distinction relates to the basis of our claims to knowledge: a judgment is *a priori* if it cannot or could not in principle be falsified by experience. Kripke wanted to show (for reasons I explain in Chapter 3) that the necessary/contingent distinction is metaphysical and not simply epistemological. He therefore needed cases where the normal pairings were reversed. For an example of a contingent *a priori* proposition, one need look no further than 'I exist' (if one believes that this is a proposition). If I know anything independently of experience, it is this, but I need not have existed. Kripke's argument derives its force from the assumed presence of a single proposition in 'The Morning Star is the Evening Star', which can be given an intensional twist.

Another intensional verb is 'to mean'. In Putnam's Twin Earth thought experiment (1973), which continues to be highly influential, we are to imagine a planet identical in every way to Earth, with the exception that its 'water' has a completely different chemical composition – XYZ instead of H_2O. The experienced properties of Twin Earth 'water' are the same as those of Earth water; they are indistinguishable to the eye and the palate. Because the experiment is set before 1750, no resident of either planet is aware of the chemical composition of their 'water': a Twin Earther uses the word 'water' in exactly the same way as an Earther. But, claimed Putnam, each means something different by it, namely XYZ and H_2O. Under these controlled, albeit thought-experimental, conditions meaning can be seen to co-vary with externality. Therefore externalism is true.

But consider these sentences:
(1) When Newton talked about water, he referred to H_2O.
(2) When Newton talked about water, he was referring to H_2O.
(3) When Newton talked about water, he meant H_2O.
(4) When Newton talked about water, he was meaning H_2O.

Although Newton cannot have known about the chemical composition of water, (2) can be accepted because 'to refer' is not an intensional verb. But what about (3)? Is it true or false? There is a certain *extensional* sense in which it is true, like the sense in which Lois was looking for Superman when she was really looking for Clark, and this is the sense to which Putnam was appealing. However, if, as I have argued, reference can properly be excised from meaning, the one who means is left with an intensional attitude, preserved in the intensional verb. Mildly paradoxical as it may sound, this would make (3) false: the Earther and his Twin would mean (intensionally) the same thing by 'water'. Conversely, before the Morning and Evening Stars were found to be identical, people meant different things by those names. Notice that (2) is preferable to (1) while (3) is preferable to (4). Something distinguishes meaning from referring to the extent that a change of tense is required between the clauses in (2). The change may signal a switch from intensional to extensional sense.

I suspect that the force of Putnam's argument draws on another factor. I would hesitate to say that even two Twin Earthers, in the strictest sense, mean the same thing when they use the word 'water', since the active intension of each will be governed by his distinctive psychological formation. This reservation will lead me to doubt whether a Twin Earther could mean the same thing by 'water' as an Earther. But since neither means H_2O, this qualification does not strengthen Putnam's case.

Wittgenstein was once discussing the logical form of propositions with the economist Piero Sraffa, who had left Mussolini's Italy for Cambridge at the invitation of Maynard Keynes. Sraffa moved his hand under his chin in a Neapolitan gesture and asked, 'What is the logical form of *that*?' The gesture means roughly 'Don't assume I'm interested in what you say.' It would be shockingly rude if directed at the President of Italy but could be playful if made at a friend. In the book that made his reputation, the *Tractatus Logico-Philosophicus*, Wittgenstein had outlined a project to create a logically perfect language (as dreamt of by Frege) that would map the observable universe through the medium of the proposition in an extensional fashion. By the time he wrote the *Philosophical Investigations*, his position had undergone a transformation. In its preface Sraffa is acknowledged as the more important of only two named influences ('I am indebted to *this* stimulus for the most consequential ideas of this book'). The emphasis was to be on how language is used rather than how it maps to the world. Sraffa's gesture was perfectly meaningful in use, at least in an Italian context, while entirely lacking in extensional purchase. Although Wittgenstein represents an antidote to the systematic tendency in philosophy, his journey is one that later philosophers have had to repeat. Unfortunately resistance is building.

Wittgenstein nevertheless bears a certain responsibility for institutionalizing the fact. The second sentence of the *Tractatus* ('The world is the totality of facts, not of things') has been hugely influential. It is also deeply misleading since facts are confined to minds. To believe otherwise is to fall prey to idealism. Unfortunately the later Wittgenstein did not repudiate the sentiment but instead dressed the fact as a socio-linguistic construction. When I said, at the end of Chapter 1, that S-theory is less conducive to anti-realism than the dominant model, I had in mind its ability to put facts in their proper place.

The propositional attitude

The intensional character of the verb 'to believe' emerges when a person believes *that* something is the case. Thus Lois might believe that Superman is very strong while believing that Clark is a bit weedy. In the sentences 'Lois believes that Superman is very strong' and 'Lois believes that Clark is a bit weedy', the names

'Superman' and 'Clark' co-refer but cannot be substituted for each other without a misrepresentation of Lois's epistemic stances. These are not contradictory, as they would be expected to be on an extensional logic. When a person 'believes *that*...', he is said to hold a *propositional attitude*. If I say 'Jack believes that Turing invented the computer', I am attributing to Jack a certain kind of psychological state. This state appears to have propositional content, the proposition in question being 'Turing invented the computer.' If Jill also believes that Turing invented the computer, she stands in a similar cognitive relation to the same proposition. Although belief is the standard propositional attitude, a person can hope, fear, regret, imagine or suspect that something is, was or will be the case. There are many other *attitudinal* verbs; their value lies in bringing others' states of mind and emotion into discourse, as well as in linking affect to psychology. When a propositional attitude is reported, its holder's point of view will be preserved whenever possible. If Turing had, unbeknownst to Jack, been ennobled as Lord Bletchley, this would not license us to say 'Jack believes that Lord Bletchley invented the computer.' This sentence would not be true.

Communication is based on our highly developed sensitivity to one another's propositional attitudes. A sentence can be meant by a speaker who does not believe it to be true, if his intention is to deceive a hearer into believing it. But if he does not intend to deceive, he cannot mean the sentence without also believing it to be true. If I were to say to you, 'The 1st of January 1800 was a Tuesday', you would have to conclude that either (a) I had established this as a fact, (b) I had established that it was not a Tuesday but was trying to deceive you or (c) that I had simply concocted the sentence and therefore did not mean it. If you went for (a), you would justifiably take my statement to reflect my belief. If I was uncertain, you would expect me to indicate this by saying 'I *think* the 1st of January 1800 was a Tuesday'. This aspect of communication underlies G. E. Moore's Paradox, as illustrated by these sentences:

(1) It's raining but I don't believe that it's raining.
(2) It's raining but he doesn't believe that it's raining.

(1) seems to involve a contradiction, whereas (2) does not. But there is no explanation in logic for the difference. We naturally read these sentences as statements or potential statements. (1) could not be used to deceive since the speaker would be giving the game away by his denial. In saying and meaning 'It's raining', he will be taken to believe that it is raining. With his denial, he therefore expresses himself in a contradictory fashion. This close connection with meaning may tell us something about the psychological nature of what we term a 'belief'.

The verb 'to know' plays a special role in propositional attitude reports. The tendency in philosophy is to treat knowledge as a superior form of belief. To be counted as knowledge, a belief must of course be true. The problem is to define what other criteria must be met. The traditional view, that it is sufficient for a belief to be true and justified, was upset by Edmund Gettier (1963). His two cases, in which beliefs were true and apparently justified but did not seem to constitute knowledge, opened the way for many more. One concerns a farmer, Bob, who wants to be sure that his cow, Daisy, is in a particular field. He goes to look and sees something black and white and quite large behind a tree. This convinces him that Daisy is in the field and he returns satisfied. In fact, what he saw was a piece of paper. Daisy is indeed in the field but was out of sight. Bob's belief is therefore true and is also justified in the sense that he had good reason to think he saw Daisy. But he cannot be said to *know* that she is in the field.

One might suppose that this is because he did not actually see her. But consider the next case. Helen is driving through a rural area where barns are common. These barns are of a type unfamiliar in Britain: they have a frontage large enough to conceal the rest of the structure from view. In this area, for reasons we can only guess at, people are given to erecting 'fake' barns, that is, barn frontages with nothing behind them. From the road they look exactly like the real barns, which they outnumber. Helen is unaware that there are fake barns. She turns a corner and sees a frontage, which happens to belong to a real barn. She forms the belief that she is looking at a barn. Her belief is both true and justified. Unlike Bob, she really is looking at a barn. But would we say that she knows that it is a barn?

If not, the reason may be that we know more about the situation than Helen. From our standpoint the truth of Helen's belief is due to chance. This makes it impossible for us endorse it as knowledge. We would not allow such a belief to enter the repository, since it would soon become a matter of chance whether the repository was reliable. This scruple is not a reflection of some deficiency in Helen's psychological state, which would be no different if there were no fake barns. We are not trying to describe that state. Rather we are endorsing, or not endorsing, the propositional attitude associated with that state. We cannot be neutral observers where knowledge is concerned. It is therefore more than a type of belief. This is unfortunate for philosophers, who need a way to investigate how we as thinking subjects can be said to know things, for example how we can have *a priori* knowledge or knowledge of the external world, including minds other than our own. The question is whether an individual, taken in isolation before the existence of other minds has been established, can meaningfully be said to know. It is rather like asking whether an individual, purely on her own terms, could be late.

Of course people often claim that they know things. But they invariably do so with a hearer in mind. Their purpose is to influence the hearer's state of awareness so that either she may accept the speaker's expressed belief or share it more unshakeably. If an individual is convinced of a truth that others reject, he will try to persuade them since his knowledge is otherwise likely to be useless, unless he can act on it alone. Alternatively, a person claiming to know something may be indicating that he has access to a piece of knowledge that is already in the repository. If I know that Mercury is the planet closest to the Sun, I do not have to justify a belief.

The price of this confidence is the subjection of shared knowledge to the highest available standards of justification, which for us are scientific. Moreover, scientific facts can only be known scientifically, in our sense of the word. Did Democritus of Abdera know that matter was composed of atoms or did he only believe it? I think he only believed it, since he could not establish such a fact in a way acceptable to us. The justificatory mechanism can be seen in the application by means of peer review of standards of methodological rigour to scientific research. The individual scientist internalizes these standards when he asks himself whether a certain inference is warranted.

If one accepts the proposition and the extensionality it implies, the propositional attitude can be used to manufacture logical problems, for example by juxtaposing Lois Lane's contradictory beliefs about the same person. A vast literature has been stimulated by these pseudo-problems, which can all be traced to referential semantics. The propositional attitude nevertheless denotes a significant psychological state, which might alternatively be described as a 'linguistically enabled attitude'. A better expression could no doubt be found. I shall stick slightly uncomfortably with 'propositional attitude', while denying that propositions exist.

Modality and apriority

Since Aristotle philosophers have been at pains to distinguish what is the case necessarily from what is merely possible or contingent. Mathematical truths seem to provide the strongest example of necessity since it is impossible to conceive of a reality in which they do not hold. Natural language has also been thought capable of expressing necessary truths, an example being the identity statement ('The moon is the moon'). Inevitably necessity or its opposite, contingency, have been attributed to the proposition, which is described as having *modal* properties. The question therefore arises: what happens to modality when the proposition is dispensed with? An answer is required since one of the foremost virtues of language, as noted above, is that it can be used to frame contingency and thereby provide leverage on the world. It is easy enough to say that what is stated by a contingent sentence could be or have been otherwise, but this merely shifts the burden of explanation from necessity to possibility.

Taking a cue from Leibniz, Kripke was largely responsible for what is now the standard view, that a necessary proposition is one that is true in all possible worlds, as we could conceive them. Signing up to the theory of possible worlds means accepting that they metaphysically exist, not merely that they might exist. Nothing limits their proliferation: there is a possible world accommodating any imaginable state of affairs. I regard this as the metaphysical conceit *par excellence* – the kind of thing that has given metaphysics a bad name and which no one should be expected to swallow even in pursuit of enlightenment. I suggest instead that necessary truths are those that strike us as *not* necessitated by cognitive conditions of satisfaction. To be so necessitated, or contingent, a sentence must contain an expression capable of isolating part of the world. This will be some kind of name.

Mathematical propositions do not contain names and therefore cannot be contingent; if true, they are true necessarily. They present themselves as not necessitated because they appear to be true independently of what anyone might conceive or mentally construct. They are not facts.

What then of sentences in natural language which are claimed by philosophers to be true necessarily? Here are some examples:

(1) The Morning Star is the Evening Star.
(2) Cilantro is coriander.
(3) Florence is Firenze.
(4) Water is H_2O.
(5) Gold is a metal.
(6) Squirrels are mammals.
(7) Bachelors are unmarried.

Even if it could be shown that one of these sentences is necessary, it would additionally have to be shown that its necessity is the same thing as the necessity of mathematical truths. It might, for example, be a kind of weakened contingency. It could have been the case that English invented a different name for Firenze; it could have been the case that water turned out to have a different composition (it was discovered in the 1930s to contain small amounts of deuterium oxide, D_2O or 'heavy water'). So contingency is present. Unlike mathematics and logic, natural language is itself a contingent phenomenon to which strict necessity is likely to be alien. The identity statement in its vacuity is the exception that proves the rule. Kripke would argue that the pairs of terms in (1) – (4) rigidly designate the same thing and therefore also form identity statements. However, by associating distinctive intension with the terms, we can make the sentences interesting (non-vacuous) under particular imaginary circumstances. In fact the verb 'to be' has a different sense in (4) from (1) – (3), casting further doubt on any logical properties they might be thought to share.

The first six examples seem necessary perhaps because they are about either naming or classification rather than about what they denote. If a system of scientific classification exists, within its frame of reference non-contingent sentences will be possible. But unlike mathematics any system of scientific classification is itself a historical contingency that is subject to revision at any time. Sentence (7) is commonly held to be *analytic*: its meaning is already contained in the meaning of 'bachelor'. This is possible because 'bachelor' is not a name – bachelors are not parsed. A state of awareness that bachelors are unmarried would not normally necessitate the sentence, since anyone who understood the word 'bachelor' would already possess that state of awareness. The sentence is therefore strongly non-contingent. Mathematical truths are also thought by some to be analytic on the grounds that, for example, 2 + 2 (or 2 and +) contains the meaning of 4. The proposition 2 + 2 = 4 is nonetheless interesting; otherwise there would be no mathematicians.

Modality also features explicitly in sentences containing the verbs 'may', 'must', 'should' and 'can'. Originally these modal verbs will have had a person as subject, as in 'Zog may come on the hunt' (I permit him), 'Zog must come' (I command him), 'Zog should come' (I oblige him) and 'Zog cannot come' (I prohibit him). There is nothing here that requires explanation. But the verbs were adapted to make sentences of the form:

(1) There may be three apples in that bag.
(2) There must be three apples in that bag.
(3) There should be three apples in that bag.
(4) There cannot be three apples in that bag.

If the speaker is trying to control what is put in the bag, he may utter these sentences with the original senses of the modal verbs, as fiats. But the sentences can also be used to express a belief about what is in the bag. If I utter and mean (1), I intend a different state of awareness in my hearer from that which would necessitate the statement 'There are three apples in that bag.' How do they differ? With any modal sentence, the speaker tries to mould his hearer's state of awareness by putting a spin on the belief that he is taken by the hearer to hold. If I uttered (2), I would be trying to impress on a hearer that there are reasons, which I accept, for discounting the possibility that there are not three apples in the bag. (4) aims at the opposite effect. In both cases I would likely adduce reasons in support of my belief. If I uttered (3), I would be trying to weight the possibility without committing myself to it, while with (1) I would merely appraise my hearer of the possible existence of a state of affairs, with the implication that I lacked or was unwilling to offer grounds for believing in it. There is no contradiction in the sentence 'It may be raining but I don't believe that it's raining.' There is a contradiction in 'It must be raining but I don't believe that it's raining.'

If necessity can be accounted for without reference to the proposition, is the same true of the *a priori/a posteriori* distinction? Apriority and aposteriority are features of judgments or claims to knowledge. A judgment is likely to be couched in a sentence. If the sentence is taken to harbour a proposition, the *a priori* or *a posteriori* status of the judgment will gravitate to the proposition. However, the capacity for judgment is arguably pre-linguistic, relating to the way in which sensory experience is assimilated and construed. Thus the differing reactions of a cat and a snake to a disappearing mouse betoken different capacities for judgment. The cat's behaviour indicates that it has benefit of a judgment to the effect that mice do not just disappear. We might generalize to 'Things don't just disappear' but our adaptive stance, albeit linguistically expressed, remains closely related to our fellow mammal's. If a person searched unsuccessfully for a set of keys, she would never give up because she had concluded that it must have disappeared into thin air. Such a judgment would not be self-contradictory but it would be inconsistent with what we all know about the world and how it works. This is the sense in which an *a priori* judgment cannot be falsified by experience. Apriority cannot be properly elucidated without reference to the evolutionary adaptation to fundamental constancies in the external world.

If the sentence 'I exist' contains a proposition, it must be the proposition also contained by the sentence 'William Reynolds exists.' But whereas 'I exist' is *a priori*, 'William Reynolds exists', unless uttered by me, is clearly *a posteriori*. It would present itself as contingent to anyone but me and could in principle be falsified by their experience. The assumption of the proposition therefore creates a contradiction.

Pragmatics

Many linguisticians share with philosophers of language an interest in the way that language can be used to convey more than, or even something quite different from, the strict semantic meaning of sentences and other expressions. We should be prepared for this to happen by the example of metaphor. I might say 'Alice is a brick', without wishing to imply that she is in fact a brick. But there are other cases where a speaker manages to communicate more to a hearer than his words appear to yield when taken in isolation, even metaphorically. I might say to a friend 'You are charm personified', when we both know I mean the opposite. The study of this mechanism and the various uses to which it is put is known as *pragmatics*. Pragmatics is commonly understood as taking over where semantics in some sense ends, the location of the boundary, and indeed how there can be a boundary, being points of debate. The position is frequently characterized in terms of the *underdetermination* of speaker's meaning by semantic meaning.

I will look at two approaches to pragmatics, as represented in the work of Paul Grice (1975) and Kent Bach (2007). Bach provides a crop of examples whose common feature is some form of elision. The words in brackets are implied without being stated:

Everyone [*in my family*] went to the wedding.
Lola had nothing [*appropriate*] to wear.
I will be there [*at the agreed time*].
Jack and Jill are married [*to each other*].
Sam doesn't have [*only*] three kids – he has four.
He's not [*what I'd call*] a shrink – he's a psychiatrist.

Bach also cites the well-known example of the word 'and'. The two sentences 'Ronnie insulted his boss and got fired' and 'Ronnie got fired and insulted his boss' could be expected to have the same meaning. Taken semantically, the word 'and' appears to be equivalent to the logical operator '&'. In propositional logic, 'P & Q' is interchangeable with 'Q & P'. However the Ronnie sentences have different meanings because the word 'and' can carry the pragmatic overtone of 'and as a result'. Bach coined the term *impliciture* to denote a pragmatic nuance not explicitly present.

Grice was primarily interested in conversational rules and the ways in which speakers can derive communicative leverage from them. In one of his examples, two people are conversing:

A: Smith doesn't seem to have a girlfriend these days.
B: He has been paying a lot of visits to New York lately.

B manages to suggest, in what Grice termed an *implicature*, that the reason for Smith's visits may be romantic. How does he do this with a remark that in itself bears no hint of this? Grice suggested that conversation is regulated by commonly understood but unstated maxims, including 'Be relevant', 'Do not say what you believe to be false', 'Do not make your contribution more informative than is required', 'Be perspicuous', 'Be orderly', 'Be brief' and 'Avoid ambiguity.' Unless B has suddenly taken leave of his senses, A must assume that he is observing the maxim of relevance, in which case his statement must be intended to imply that Smith could have a girlfriend in New York. B knows that A will interpret his statement in this way, so the conversation can continue smoothly.

In Bach's pragmatics, the speaker relies on established usage to abbreviate his statement, in such a way that meaning is preserved. When it is stated that X and Y are married, it is implied by convention that they are married to each other. Curiously the truth value of an abbreviated sentence ('Lola had nothing to wear') may be different from the one to which it unpacks ('Lola had nothing appropriate to wear'): if its meaning were truth-conditional, we might expect some faint sense of contradiction. Be that as it may, the speaker adds nothing by meaning these sentences as statements that is not already available by convention in their expressed meaning. In Grice's pragmatics by contrast the speaker is free to aim for a unique effect: it is possible that no one has ever used B's remark to imply what he wishes to imply. Because all conversations are different, the scope for the imaginative exploitation of expectation is unlimited.

Can S-theory throw light on pragmatics? The standard explanation of what is happening is less than convincing. The sentence resembles a message that travels between the speaker and the hearer, as if down a telephone line, while retaining its strict semantic content. This explicit meaning somehow conceals or encodes an additional implicit meaning intended for the hearer, who cleverly decodes or 'recovers' it at her end. Of course many utterances are directed at multiple hearers or at an audience unknown to the speaker. They may nevertheless contain implicit meaning as long as the speaker is confident that he is communicating successfully.

When a cognitivist uses the term 'underdetermination', he invariably indicates an explanatory gap. To the S-theorist however it is an encouraging telltale sign. What would happen if we were to interpret 'speaker's meaning' as the condition of satisfaction of his meant utterance in the hearer's state of awareness?

Underdetermination would then describe the causal insufficiency of the utterance as satisfaciend. I suggest that speakers are under pressure to make their utterances fully necessitated, which gives rise to the appearance of underdetermination. Speakers have many ways of minimizing their satisfaciend utterances. A pronoun will be substituted for a noun if meaning is not compromised. One can reply to a question without having to repeat it as a sentence. The expression 'Don't count your chickens before they're hatched' is rarely heard nowadays because everyone just says 'Don't count your chickens.' This may in time be superseded by 'Don't count them.' Speakers are expected to be economical and elegant, on pain of being boring or even of being thought unhinged. The overall effect is the phenomenon in question – the semantic shortfall.

Bach's and Grice's versions illustrate different types of opportunity for minimization. Grice saw that Wittgenstein's point about meaning as use had a wider application than isolated expressions. Some of his conversational maxims actually reduce to the minimization requirement, with 'Avoid ambiguity' acting as a backstop. Conversation is modulated according to the speaker's familiarity with the hearer, which creates further opportunities for minimization and the introduction of esoteric meaning, which we all seem to appreciate.

Conversational behaviour is a rich seam. Suppose that Jack and Jill are hurrying to get ready to go out, but Jill can't find her car keys. She claims to have looked everywhere. In a tone of voice familiar to Jill, Jack says, 'Things don't just disappear.' Taken in isolation, this sentence expresses an *a priori* judgment. So why, at this critical moment, should Jack choose to deliver one of those? Why, for that matter, should Jill take umbrage at it? Because he is using it to imply that she is at fault in either mislaying the keys or failing to find them, or both. Jack can achieve this effect because he knows that Jill's awareness that things don't just disappear does not necessitate his statement. Because the statement cannot therefore be meant at face value, it must be meant in some other way on the general principle that people mean something when they speak. The same principle would apply to any statement whose semantic content was already known by the speaker to be known to the hearer, but a contingent sentence could not carry the requisite force. Given the operation of Grice's rule that one should be no more informative than is necessary, Jack can inject sarcasm or reproach by being non-contingently over-informative.

Is there then a boundary between semantics and pragmatics? The question is too complex to be answered on the basis of a cursory review. Semantics is largely concerned with the emergence of meaning from syntactic structure. At a low level it can probably be separated from the higher, psychological reaches of pragmatics. However, nowhere along this spectrum is a clean break possible. If underdetermination is intrinsic to semantics, and pragmatics almost always relies on semantic content (silence can have pragmatic significance), it may be more useful to treat them as two sides of the same coin. Needless to say, pragmatics is alien to mathematical propositions.

Speech acts

Taking Wittgenstein's insight in a slightly different direction, J. L. Austin (1962) and John Searle (1969) developed the theory of speech acts, classifying them under a few broad headings according to what they are intended to achieve. The *directive*, for example, is normally an imperative and is aimed at getting another person to do something. The *assertive* is the standard declarative sentence, while the *expressive* covers a ragbag of expressions, such as 'Congratulations!', 'Sorry', 'Shame!', 'Thank you' and 'What a beautiful day!' Expressives seem to denote a certain disposition, as opposed to a belief, in the speaker, which he wishes to convey to the hearer. Many single-word expressives seem to be abbreviations of sentences ('I congratulate you'). An utterance such as 'I love you' has the form of a declarative sentence but the communicative significance of an expressive. 'How interesting!' is not the recommended reply.

The category I want to consider here is the *commissive*, which includes promises and threats. A feature of speech act theory, which is not developed in pragmatics, is that certain conditions must be met for an utterance to count as a speech act. These are Searle's conditions for a promise:

(1) The propositional content of the promise-utterance represents some future action A by speaker S.
(2) Hearer H prefers S's doing A to his not doing it, and S believes that H would prefer his doing A to his not doing it.
(3) It is not obvious to S or H that S will do A in the normal course of events.
(4) S intends to do A (later amended to: S intends that his utterance will make him responsible for intending to do A).
(5) S intends that his utterance will place him under an obligation to do A.
(6) S intends that his utterance will produce in H a belief that conditions (4) and (5) obtain by means of the recognition of the intention to produce that belief, and he intends this recognition to be achieved by means of the recognition of the sentence as one conventionally used to produce such beliefs.

These six *constitutive* conditions are part of the meaning, for Searle, of a promise. He also maintains that the condition of satisfaction of a promise is the intention to perform the corresponding action. This is unlikely to be an S-type condition of satisfaction since an intention does not normally necessitate a promise by the person intending. A limitation of Searle's account is that, despite appearing exhaustive, it is all about future action by the speaker. But a speaker could promise that something will happen over which he has no control, for example that the weather will be fine in Peru in February. Is it legitimate to treat this type of promise as somehow metaphorical?

As the name might suggest, speech act theory will inevitably intersect with an S-based approach to utterances. The fact that assertive speech acts have, on S-theory, conditions of satisfaction in states of awareness suggests that other types of speech act may have similar conditions of satisfaction. For example, the purpose of a threat would appear to be to induce a state of fear. Unless he pays his debt, Len could threaten to tell Ken's wife about it, leaving Ken with a 'fear that', namely the fear that Len will tell his wife. Ken's fear necessitates Len's threat. Len might then promise Ken that he will let him off if Bombardier wins the 3.30 at Newmarket. How should we characterize Ken's new propositional attitude? The obvious choice is as a hope: normally the content of the hope would be the promised action, but since in this case the action is conditional on Bombardier's win, that eventuality becomes the content of Ken's hope. The hope necessitates the promise since Ken would have no reason to hope had Len not made the promise, but the promise does not determine the hope's content. If Ken happens to know that Bombardier does well with a certain jockey, he will no doubt hope that the jockey is riding.

A promise could therefore be an utterance which has a 'hope that' as its condition of satisfaction. It may be a hope that the weather will be fine in Peru in February. Not all hopes necessitate promises – they may be spontaneous. When a person makes a promise, he intentionally induces a hope. If I say 'I will be in London on Friday', aware that the effect of my words will be a hope, my utterance is a *de facto* promise, even if I do not make this explicit. Intention is essential since a stray remark could give rise to a hope; the explicit use of the word 'promise' obviates any misunderstanding. But the intention to induce a hope should be distinguished from any intention to perform a promise-fulfilling action. Promising can be entirely cynical. Contrary to Searle's fourth condition, a person could make a promise and intentionally induce a hope without intending to fulfil it (or to make himself responsible for anything). He could not deny having made a promise on the grounds that he never intended to fulfil it.

The main philosophical puzzle about promising is how a form of words can create an obligation, even when the promise is implicit. Obligations are normally created by circumstances, for example when a person borrows a sum of money. Suppose that when Len starts to get impatient, Ken promises to repay the debt.

Ken cannot at that point be creating the obligation to repay the debt since it must have come into existence when he borrowed the money. So what is the additional obligatory character of the promise? If a promise that the weather in Peru will be fine is a genuine promise, why is the weather not obliged to be fine? I suggest that rather than pertaining to the promiser's future action, if there is one, obligation pertains to the induced hope. It would be more accurate to describe it as a responsibility for the hope, on the principle that a dashed hope is an injury. In other words, one should not promise unless one can guarantee to one's own satisfaction that the resulting hope will not be dashed, leaving one responsible for an injury. This need not involve an action. On the other hand a promiser may find that in order to prevent a hope from being dashed, far more is required of him than he or the beneficiary originally envisaged. He might, for example, have to travel 1000 miles instead of 10.

Because the promised action is not the *locus* of obligation, it will likely cease to be obligatory if its non-performance will not cause the induced hope to be dashed. I might promise to bring a potato salad to your party but subsequently discover that Harriet, whose potato salad is even better than mine, intends to make one, unbeknownst to you. I would still be obliged to bring something but not a potato salad. Making a promise to a child carries a particular kind of obligation because the dashing of the hope may have less quantifiable psychological repercussions than it would in an adult.

A form of promising seems to occur when a person commits himself to the reciprocation of a benefit. Thus Ben might undertake to mend Den's car in return for Den's mending of Ben's computer. Ben's action in mending Den's car is not like a loan since it does not automatically create an obligation: people do not always expect something in return for a service. However, the understanding on this occasion is that Den will reciprocate, so an obligation is created. Suppose that Den then fails to reciprocate. He will have reneged on the obligation to reciprocate but will he also have broken an implicit promise? The obligation will have caused Ben to hold a material expectation, just as it would if he had lent Den money. Unlike a hope, a material expectation is not the condition of satisfaction of a speech act. When a material obligation is not met, the result is more likely to be a grievance than the dashing of a hope. Nevertheless, if the form of words used by Den in contracting the obligation also caused Ben to hope, he will have made a *de facto* promise and added to his obligation. In my view this would be the case even if Den was unaware that he was inducing a hope, since he should have been: that is, undertaking to reciprocate a benefit is likely to be hope-inducing, as declaring that one will be in London on Friday is not.

Why then do people make promises? Clearly their motives may be self-interested. Promising a future benefit is likely to bring about a favourable and perhaps compliant attitude toward the promiser on the part of the beneficiary. But a person might also wish, for disinterested reasons, to encourage another in a course of action, knowing that a hope would contribute to her motivation.

A note on art

A category of phenotypic extension deserving of special mention is the work of art. Art can be both permanent and, if it relies on performance, in a sense ephemeral. In either case the work of art appears to have no purpose other than as art. But if it lacks purpose, it is usually held to communicate something to the looker or listener, whether or not this corresponds to something consciously intended by artist or performer. Works of art therefore resemble female phenotypic extensions in that their conditions of satisfaction do not consist in alterations to the physical state of the world. But female extensions such as maps and clocks are obviously functional. Do works of art in fact have conditions of satisfaction?

In my view they do so to the extent that they have artistic meaning for us. They will normally have immediate perceptual meaning: a painting hanging on a wall will be parsed as an art object. But it may lack artistic meaning for a given observer.

Artistic meaning is somehow more private than linguistic meaning; works of art do not prompt states of awareness convertible to information-bearing sentences. The states they prompt may not be entirely conscious but may rather have affective or emotional attributes linking them to the subconscious. The centrality of affect in the human psyche will inevitably have brought into existence artefacts with the power to evoke it. Such artefacts will have been granted extraordinary, even totemic, status within primitive cultures; some will have acquired religious significance. With time they would become a measure of civilization.

Decorative art beautifies functional phenotypic extensions such as vases and carpets, whose power to evoke affect may be compromised by their obvious utility. Non-decorative visual art often owes its effect to its resistance to straightforward parsing, giving rise to what has been termed *cognitive dissonance*. Bombarded by lifelike images, it is difficult for us to imagine the effect on our forebears of comparatively scarce realistic representation. Its fascination will have been enhanced by the compression of reference: especially in painting there was great scope for allusion and for engaging the entire mental formation of the viewer.

It may be worth mentioning that art provides our main evidence for perceptual experience at variance with our own. When we look at representations of the human form from, for example, the pre-classical period in Greece or pre-Columbian Mesoamerica, we are aware of a lack of realism. This was remedied in the Greek case during the classical period, just as philosophers were turning their attention to the human being. But there is no reason why artists of a particular time and place should be unable to achieve realism. A possible inference is that, allowing for stylistic convention, the human form was actually perceived differently. In a related way the discovery of perspective in art may have altered ordinary perception.

In the nineteenth century a crisis was provoked by photography, which rendered representation commonplace.

Ironically, if David Hockney (2001) is right, artists had been covertly using lenses and other optical aids for centuries in order to achieve realistic effects. Many responded to photography by abandoning realism in pursuit of new types of cognitive dissonance. Abstract and expressionist painting played with the binding and parsing processes, against the background of a kind of arms race with the viewing public's diminishing capacity for surprise. A significant step, and arguably the first 'conceptual art', was Marcel Duchamp's appropriation of manufactured phenotypic extensions, most famously a urinal laid flat. The dissonance would have been less marked had he chosen female extensions. Conceptual and other artists subsequently invented many more ways of disconcerting perceptual construal. However, on a narrow and pessimistic view of the future of visual art, the viewing public is bound to win the arms race, at which juncture art will lose all point. On a less pessimistic view, the new conditions will allow more freedom to the great artists of the future, whose achievements will always confound expectation and extrapolation.

Literary art felt the reverberations of the representational crisis in visual art but it had no comparable crisis of its own. We should therefore be affected by poetry much as our literate forebears were; the dividing line, if there is one, would separate us from those who only ever *heard* poetry. If poetry has artistic meaning, it must somehow ride on linguistic meaning. But on S-theory there is both expressed and realized meaning. Could it be that poetry exploits the distinction? If so, poetic diction would describe the combination of words in such a way that their meaning is realized at the affective rather than the cognitive level. This could be achieved in various ways, some of which are related to metaphor. Firstly a mythical or imaginary context could be developed in which sentences were under no obligation to reflect reality or even to sustain a coherent alternative. Secondly this freedom would provide scope for ambiguity of meaning, placing the burden of interpretation on the hearer/reader and thereby stimulating psychological processes that could in turn evoke affect. Thirdly words could be deployed in unfamiliar combinations or without conformity to normal rules, thereby loosening up or confounding habitual patterns of construal. Fourthly regular and irregular poetic rhythms and rhymes could be used to evoke affective responses associated with music and dance.

The most mysterious art form is considered by many to be music. Its abstraction makes a theory of cognitive dissonance seem inapplicable: the realized meaning of sound is perceptually and cognitively unambiguous. However, unlike visual inputs, which are organized by the brain, auditory inputs may already exhibit a form of organization. Pythagoras is credited with the discovery that harmonious musical intervals correlate with frequency ratios (string length ratios when tension is uniform) that can be expressed in whole numbers. Music exploits this natural system, which, it has to be assumed, is represented in the structure of our auditory apparatus. So although sound may be perceptually unambiguous, music is more than an agglomeration of sound. It is a kind of superstructure resting on the infrastructure of natural harmonics. Given that the infrastructure is fixed, effects can be achieved by manipulating the superstructure, which displays historically evolving formal attributes analogous with those of architecture. Indeed on classical architectural principles, traceable through Vitruvius to Pythagoras, there is a unity between proportion and harmonics.

The music of J. S. Bach offers perhaps the most profound exploration of the relation of superstructure to infrastructure. I take just two examples. Firstly he often creates a breathtaking progression through a series of keys that stretches superstructural form, as he understood it, to its limit before arriving triumphantly at his starting point. Secondly, as the greatest master of counterpoint, he constructs the most elaborate of superstructures from separate lines, each with an independent relationship to the infrastructure as melody. In this way any easy harmonic borrowing from the infrastructure is ruled out. The form that advertises this demanding technique most clearly is the fugue.

In defence of a prejudice, I would claim that the abandonment of natural tonality by a minority of twentieth-century composers was partly due to a mistaken analogy with visual art. Any crisis in music will be self-inflicted, like the one that overtook architecture in the nineteenth century, when classical principles were junked in favour of xenophobic medievalist nostalgia.

Non-human naming

Finally I would like to pay tribute to all chimpanzees and bonobos involved in language-learning experiments. The basic activity is the association of words or signs with objects or representations of objects. In other words, the animals are taught the behaviour of naming. Some have succeeded in mastering up to 500 vocabulary items in this way. Encouraged by rewards, primate subjects are adept at associative learning. But does this genuinely resemble human naming? Many cognitive scientists think not and regard these experiments as pointless. They may be the academic equivalent of the chimpanzees' tea party. Success stories may understate the extent to which the animals use their 'language' skills to demand food: they are capable of converting the naming game into a much more interesting signalling game. It would clearly be confusing if their signals were not allowed to find their behavioural conditions of satisfaction in the provision of specified food items, but compliance can only confirm to them that they are indeed in a signalling game. When they are given words, they respond most naturally if they can construe them as signals with conditions of satisfaction in their own behaviour. A good test would be an experiment in which animals were obliged to use names when communicating with one another.

Failing that, it would be more interesting to find a species whose normal behaviour can only be explained on the hypothesis that genuine naming is taking place. Constantine Slobodchikoff (2009) has for many years been observing the prairie dog *Cynomys gunnisoni* in the US Southwest. A rodent of the squirrel family which lives in large underground colonies, it has a call which sounds like canine barking; thus the name. Prairie dogs issue different types of call in reaction to the presence of different intruders above ground. Slobodchikoff has recorded these vocalizations and analyzed their acoustic structure by means of Fast-Fourier transform. Like vervets, prairie dogs have calls for different predators, which elicit different escape behaviours, but they also have calls for non-predators such as cows and deer. The latter typically do not prompt a behavioural response. Calls are modified to correlate with colour, size and shape, for example with the colour of clothes worn by human intruders. If the intruder is carrying a gun, the call will be modified accordingly (prairie dogs have been systematically persecuted by farmers). But even when objects are introduced which the animals could never have seen before, calls seem to have been invented which are similar across dispersed colonies.

Naming should not be regarded as the only criterion for language. Linguisticians have proposed a set of criteria, including syntactic articulation, that is, the construction of complex expressions from semantic components, and displacement, whereby subject matter can be handled when it is not in the visual field. Slobodchikoff's approach is to test these criteria one by one, insofar as the vocalizations can be interpreted.

Why have his findings elicited so little interest? He attributes this partly to species separation: we find it easier to grant cognitive abilities to primate than to non-primate species. It may also be the case that what prairie dogs do when they communicate does not seem sufficiently different from what bonobos can do under controlled conditions and what vervets do in the wild to warrant special attention. A clearer functional distinction between signalling and naming might help to remedy this state of affairs. Slobodchikoff also suggests that biologists have bought into the idea that controlled experimentation is the only way to obtain valid biological data. I'll let biologists sort that one out. Meanwhile, we should at least prepare ourselves for the possibility that we are not the only language users.

CHAPTER 3

THEY THOUGHT THEY WERE MACHINES

The behaviour of animals is more available to observation than what goes on inside their brains and nervous systems. Philosophers might therefore be expected to take less interest in human behaviour than in human psychology. However, the fact that behaviour is rooted in the brain makes it impossible to separate them. On the one hand behaviour is our principal means of understanding the mind, on the other hand we rely on some kind of psychological theory to interpret one another's behaviour. Evolution has left us acutely sensitive in this respect by developing traits seen in other primates. It has also made our behaviour amenable: we are able to organize collective endeavour towards a goal which has been consciously rather than instinctively grasped, and expressed by means of language. Amenability suggests that the springs of human behaviour may be linked to the cognitive impact of language.

At certain levels our behaviour is comparable with that of other animals since it originates in common biological imperatives and impulses. These normally present as *appetitive desires* – otherwise they risk being ignored. Appetitive desires are the simplest type of satisfaciend: their generic conditions of satisfaction *are* their satisfaction. If I am thirsty, I have a desire whose condition of satisfaction is the quenching of my thirst, not merely an act of drinking. I might frame my desire as a desire for a glass of water but this is only its means of satisfaction.

Being a satisfaciend, my desire is causally insufficient to find its condition of satisfaction. That depends also on the availability of its means of satisfaction in my environment. I am not powerless: I can behave with a view to locating and obtaining the means of satisfaction of my desire. My behaviour then serves my desire. My dog has also learned where water can be found and this knowledge guides him in a similar way when he is thirsty. Neither of us is committed in advance to drinking the water we locate; we might find it unpalatable. Non-appetitive desires, such as the desire for a new mobile phone, are peculiarly human and have specific content in representations of external objects. If the desire for a new mobile phone were a satisfaciend, its condition of satisfaction would not be a mobile phone but the desire's quenching, as it were. There is something tenuous about a desire whose content is epistemological: unlike that of thirst-quenching, the physiological effect of its condition of satisfaction cannot be measured. It would therefore be safer to limit the status of satisfaciend to appetitive desires.

Intention

What then distinguishes my goal-directed behaviour from that of my dog? While he has learnt to adapt his behaviour, I can conceptualize how I would need to behave in order to satisfy a novel desire. I can learn from others how they satisfy similar desires and adjust my strategy according to the circumstances I find myself in. This flexibility depends on the ability to form propositional attitudes in respect of my desire, its possible means of satisfaction and my means of choosing between them. If I am thirsty in the middle of a strange town on a weekday afternoon, I may decide that my best option is to look for a shop that sells bottled water, believing that such a shop is likely to exist. I consequently form an *intention* to buy a bottle of water. My intention is a type of propositional attitude with a unique relation to a piece of behaviour, which it in some way prefigures.

Human behaviour is therefore less Pavlovian and more difficult to explain than that of other animals. The central paradox is that on the one hand there is an idea, for example the idea of the purchase of a bottle of water, and on the other a physical event (my walking into a shop) that is only explicable with reference to the idea. How these are connected is something of a mystery for reasons already discussed. No explanation is available for the causation of the behaviour by the conscious idea. Moreover the idea need not result in the behaviour: two individuals might hold the same intention but only one of them might follow it through, with no quantifiable factor inhibiting the other. This is easier to imagine if the intention is prompted by a non-appetitive desire, as it may well be.

The fact that the 'propositional' content of an intention can be characterized as information superficially lends weight to a cognitivist approach to behaviour. Computation offers a model in which, depending on programming, information can be used to drive physical processes, such as the responses of a robot to particular inputs. However, the mechanisms of the computational model are not biological and therefore cannot conduct meaning, which, as I hope to show, is an essential aspect of the conversion of intention to behaviour.

Attempts have been made to portray intention as a 'desire/belief complex'. It would appear to be the case that if I intend to do something, I believe that I shall do it. If the element of belief is synthesized in some way with a desire, the desire might account for the conversion of the complex into a behavioural impulse. A distinctively human capacity would give point to a pre-linguistic pattern. However, intention does not entail a corresponding belief. I could intend and set off to meet Alice this evening while believing that she is unlikely to venture out in such vile weather. Because I cannot contact her, I have to go, but I do not do so with the intention of standing forlornly on a street corner, as I believe is my probable fate.

People are often torn between conflicting desires. If desire were decisive in the production of behaviour, we might expect the strongest desire to prevail automatically. But intuition suggests that, no matter how powerful the desire, we are capable of resisting its force by what is termed an 'act of will'. This in turn implies that something called the 'will' may be responsible for converting intention to behaviour. Unfortunately the will is no more amenable to analysis than intention; when added to the mix, it introduces a further complicating factor. It seems to be absent when an intention meets no conflicting impulse. The problem of intention indicates a role for philosophy since, even with a complete scientific explanation of the production of behaviour, we would not necessarily understand why we think and talk about it as we do.

Let's try to clarify the relation between an intention and its corresponding behaviour. Suppose that Jack forms the intention to wash his yellow socks. While he's at work, Jill spontaneously decides to wash them. He had the intention and the thing intended happens. But is this what Jack had in mind when he intended to wash the socks? Not really: that requires that he do it himself. Well, suppose that he forms the intention to wash his yellow socks, but when he loads the machine, he forgets all about them. However, when he empties it, he finds that the socks had got mixed up with the other stuff. He had the intention and he does what he intended to do, so is this what Jack had in mind when he intended to do it? Not exactly: he must be aware that he is doing it. So: he forms the intention to wash his yellow socks, with this in mind he puts them in the machine with some other stuff, he switches on the machine, he hears it starting up, he kisses Jill and leaves for work. Half an hour later the machine breaks down, Jill calls the repairman, who comes and fixes it, she switches it on again and it completes its cycle. Is this what Jack had in mind when he intended to wash his socks? Almost: but he needs to see the whole thing through.

Even when these conditions are apparently met, a piece of behaviour may not be intended. Suppose that Alan is fed up with hearing about Jim's golfing prowess and feels an irresistible urge to drop the fragile glass trophy Jim has handed him. As the urge turns into an intention, Alan suddenly realizes the effect the breakage would have on Jim. He becomes so nervous that his hand shakes and the trophy slips through his fingers. He can honestly say that he did not mean to drop it, despite having had the intention and doing what he intended to do. Jim gives the impression of believing him.

A further complication relates to an agent's realism in intending. Imagine that Tim is playing golf. He has the worst handicap in the club. He tees off hopefully, aiming in the general direction of the green. To his and everyone else's astonishment, the ball drops into the hole. Could he have intended to hit a hole in one? We might feel that to hold an intention a person must be reasonably justified in believing that he is capable of fulfilling it without luck. Although Tim was aiming in the direction of the hole, never having previously hit a hole in one he may not even have had this outcome in mind.

People often say that they intend to do things that they cannot finally control. A politician might encourage his supporters by saying that he intended to win the coming election, or a businessman might say that he intended to become a millionaire by the age of thirty. The intention signifies commitment and readiness for effort but it is arguably rhetorical. 'I intend to' here seems to be equivalent to 'I will try (my best) to'.

If Tim could not have intended to hit a hole in one, does it follow that his hole in one was unintentional? Apparently not. This paradox is also evident in the next case. Jack can tell that Jill is asleep. He must get up at 5.30 a.m. to catch a flight, he has no confidence in his alarm clock and wants to check the time. To do this he must turn on the light. He knows that this will wake Jill. He nevertheless turns it on, whereupon she wakes up. An exchange takes place: 'I didn't mean to wake you'; 'Yes, but you knew you would.' Does he intend to wake her? Does he wake her intentionally? There seems to be no contradiction in the answers being respectively No and Yes, since it would be inaccurate to say that he wakes her unintentionally. Neither does he wake her accidentally. If the consequence of behaviour is not unintentional or accidental, it would seem that it must be intentional, even if it was not specifically intended.

Action, intension and motor behaviour

Both Alan and Jack say in their defence that they did not *mean* to do something. Meaning here seems to be synonymous with intending. Normally this would not advance analysis since the notion of meaning to do something would itself need explaining. But we happen to have a theory of meaning. Can we by any chance find an S-axis in intended behaviour? If an intention were a satisfaciend, it would have a condition of satisfaction in the intended behaviour but would not be causally sufficient to bring it about. Let's call the behavioural condition of satisfaction an *action*. An action would thus necessitate an intention, implying that an action could not be performed by an agent incapable of holding a propositional attitude, for example a dog. I doubt that anyone would want to defend the notion that animals perform actions. A machine may be said to have an 'action' but this can simply be treated as another use of the word.

The scope of action can therefore be limited to human behaviour. The task is then to establish that in the cases described above action correlates robustly with intention. If the concept of an action is wider than that of an intention, there may be actions that do not necessitate intentions, which would count against the presence of an S-axis, at least as postulated. It seems that Jack never quite succeeds in performing the action of washing his socks. When Alan drops the trophy or if the politician succeeds in winning the election, neither exactly qualifies as an action. Tim's hole in one, on the other hand, at first sight does seem to qualify, as does Jack's waking of Jill. It looks as though an action can be merely intentional and not intended; it is just that the intention (to tee off towards the hole or to turn on the light) may have a different description from that of the action (hitting a hole in one or waking Jill).

Jack might take an opposing view: he might deny that his waking of Jill was an action. He might object that an action must be described in a manner recognizable to the agent as that in which he framed his intention. 'Jack woke Jill by turning the light on' would not, according to Jack, describe his action, even though it might be a way of describing what happened. On another occasion, when Jill had to get up early and had asked him to wake her, Jack might say that the same sentence did properly describe his action.

He would be indicating two different uses of the verb 'to wake', one of which is intensional. The intensional sense is like the sense in which Lois was looking for Clark but not for Superman. Just as *in an extensional sense* she was looking for Superman, Jack in an extensional sense woke Jill by turning the light on to check the time, or washed his yellow socks by accident. The extensional sense of behavioural verbs describes what happens independently of the agent's point of view. A verb used extensionally therefore cannot express the subject's intention. If a verb is to denote an action, it must have an intensional sense. An intensional verb such as 'to look for' by default reflects the subject's point of view and cannot be used extensionally without misrepresentation. I would say that it was not the case that Lois was looking for Superman. Jack, however, would have difficulty in claiming that Jill's assertion that he woke her was false, since the verb 'to wake' is not an intensional verb.

Suppose that Jack says to himself before turning on the light to check the time, 'I am going to wake Jill.' Because he does not intend to wake her, this utterance would count as a *prediction*, just as it would if he were talking of another person.

A single behavioural event may be given multiple descriptions, some intensional and others extensional. In a famous example, Sally comes home one evening and switches on the light in her sitting room, thereby inadvertently surprising a burglar. Sally (a) switched on the light and (b) surprised a burglar. Only (a) is an action: only in (a) is the verb intensional. This is not because the surprising of the burglar is a consequence of the switching on of the light. If Sally had known the burglar was there, she could have performed the action of surprising him by doing exactly what she did. When an action has consequences, intended or unintended, they can often be used to characterize or redescribe the action itself. But if the consequence of an action is unintended, its use as a description of the action will be extensional, and an action cannot be described extensionally.

If a verb describes an action, its intensional sense ascribes a corresponding intention to the subject. However, nothing explicitly indicates that a behavioural verb is being used intensionally. Most of the time we don't seem to find it a problem to infer this from context. We habitually describe the behaviour of other animals as if we were ascribing intention, even when we know better. When describing human behaviour, we tolerate ambiguity: we are content simply to say that Tim hit a hole in one. Economy of expression appears to have won out over an alternative scenario in which intensionality is explicitly flagged, perhaps for reasons of pragmatic minimization. But suppose Sally's burglar suffered a heart attack on being surprised. It might then need to be established whether she surprised him intentionally, since this would be relevant to the question of her responsibility. Jill might sufficiently annoy Jack by telling a friend that he woke her up that he might want to make her extensional usage explicit. We commonly exploit for effect the fact that an action may have unintended consequences. For example, if someone said 'Sally put a strain on the emergency services that night', any irony would derive from the telescoping of unintended consequences to a verb that sounds, but cannot be, intensional.

A person can intend not only to do something but also to be something. I might intend to weigh fourteen stone by this time next year or to be better at tennis, outcomes entirely within my control. But where is the action? We could take the course of extending the concept of action to include personal states. But it seems to me more natural to say that I intend to *get* my weight down or to *improve* my tennis. Intending to be something, for example Prime Minister, may also fall foul of the condition that the intender should have a degree of control. Actions need not involve overt activity: one can intend to listen to a piece of music. A person can also intend not to do something, for example not to vote at the next election. But an appropriate verb of action, such as 'to abstain', is normally available.

Imagine a person driving a car and making a series of movements in order to turn the steering wheel, change gear and apply the brakes. Would we describe these movements as actions? Motor behaviour consists of an incalculable number of tiny muscle movements. At a certain level of fine-grainedness one must cease to be aware of their individuation. This would imply that one also ceases to be in conscious control of them. But, as indicated in Chapter 1, conscious control of motor behaviour is an illusion created by the fact that we recognize it to be accurate, its accuracy having been developed by means of conscious feedback. The fine-grained muscle movements that make up motor behaviour are therefore coordinated and meant pre-consciously. This is manifest in the behaviour of an experienced driver: she can engage in conversation without being distracted from the task in hand. Her movements do not necessitate conscious intentions and are therefore not actions. She might change down in order to go up a hill, but the fact that she could, if asked, give a reason for changing down does not imply that it was an action.

Motor behaviour is one of the animal brain's dual conditions of satisfaction. If we observe a spider in motion, we witness a form of meant behaviour. The spider's movements are autonomously, neurologically governed as they would not be if someone were to make it move by attaching threads to its legs and pulling them. Our motor behaviour has the same kind of neurological basis in pathways hammered out by practice. When we engage in an extended activity like driving a car, we rely on unconscious control of our muscles by the brain, depending on how practised we are.

Because language has in our case been superimposed on the efferent neurology common to organisms with a nervous system, we should not be surprised to find problems of definition where consciously intended action shades into pre-consciously initiated motor behaviour. We tend, for example, to think of a conscious, active person as being in a continuous intentional state. A person who is driving a car is likely to have formed an intention to go somewhere. But we cannot always tell from her movements whether they represent meant behaviour or intended action. Compare two drivers, one a learner and the other experienced. Most of the learner's behaviour is pre-conceived. For example, when he comes to a hill, he remembers that he needs to change down and forms an intention to do so. The experienced driver, on the other hand, changes down as it were unconsciously, without forming an intention. The learner's transition to the state where he no longer needs to form an intention to change down will be gradual. To do something while meaning to do it is therefore not necessarily to do it while consciously intending to do it. A verb that describes meant behaviour rather than intended action will also have an intensional sense. If a commentary could be run on the experienced driver's behaviour, it would contain sentences like 'Now she's changing down.' The intension of the verb would reflect the intension of the driver's meant behaviour, which is common to other animals unable to form conscious intentions. The sentence as uttered also contains the semantic intension of the speaker, provided it is meant as a statement. Speech acts are a form of motor behaviour and emerge from the unconscious bearing linguistic intension. A speech act may be an action, if the speaker has formed a prior intention to commit it, but the intension of a statement is at root the intension of motor behaviour. The condition of satisfaction of a speech act is mediated by the phenomenal consciousness of another person: what is a behavioural S-axis for the speaker prompts a cognitive S-axis in the hearer, which depends on a perceptual S-axis from the hearer's brain to his auditory experience.

The conversion with practice of intended action to meant behaviour may have a wider significance. When a child learns to tell the time, he does so by means of sentences: the state of the clock is represented to him linguistically. The female extension's cognitive condition of satisfaction is mediated by language in the first instance. But when telling the time becomes routine, assimilation does not depend on our forming sentences about it, although this is how we would express our awareness. I want to say that an adult can look at a clock and grasp the time without the intervention of language. Because the brain is always under pressure to streamline habitual processes, linguistic components, like any others, are squeezed. As they are streamlined, habitual processes have a diminishing claim on consciousness. This raises the question of what happens in the brain when awareness that is originally language-enabled becomes habitual and marginalized in consciousness. This is the kind of issue where philosophy has an interest but lacks its own analytical tools.

The distinction between the intentional and the accidental or unintentional is sometimes confused with the distinction between the voluntary and the involuntary. We use the term 'involuntary' in two senses. A person may lack control over his motor behaviour, for example when he sneezes or shivers, or he may lack control or autonomy over an intention. He may be forced to do something that he would not choose to do, while retaining control of his motor behaviour in the process. A sailor condemned to walk the plank might prefer to do it without assistance. This would qualify as an action necessitating an intention: his utterance – 'I am going to walk the plank' – would not be a prediction. But his action would not be voluntary, since his intention would be coerced. When a person sneezes or shivers, his motor behaviour is involuntary and therefore cannot belong to an action ('to sneeze' is never intensional). So there is involuntary action and involuntary motor behaviour. Involuntary action is intended of necessity. If motor behaviour is not involuntary it must be meant. We often use the word 'intentional' here for 'meant'; we cannot always know whether an intention was formed. But meant motor behaviour is not always adequate to the task: the result may be an accident, such as the breaking of a fragile object. The subject may then be said to have dropped the object accidentally. Here the verb 'to drop' cannot be intensional; arguably one can never drop an object intensionally (one could let it drop). An action may also have an unfortunate consequence but, because intention is involved, the consequence will not be accidental but either intentional or unintentional. The difference depends on whether the agent could be expected to foresee the consequence, so an intentional consequence need not have formed part of his intention. There is an onus on agents to foresee, and by implication take responsibility for, the consequences of their actions. 'Unintentional' therefore has an exonerating sense.

Reasons for action

When people perform actions, they usually have reasons as well as intentions. Jack might buy Jill flowers for one or more reasons. Because intentions are rightly seen as causally insufficient for actions, philosophers who propose or anticipate a causal theory of action may instead hypothesize reasons as causes of action. This approach is associated in particular with Donald Davidson (1963). The picture is complicated by the fact that there are at least three types of reason for action. Firstly there may be a circumstantial reason, such as its being Jill's birthday or Jack's having an early flight to catch. Secondly there may be a motivational reason: Jack loves Jill and is conscientious about his work. Thirdly there may be a teleological reason: Jack buys flowers *in order to* give Jill a nice surprise, he turns on the light in order to check the time. Now there is a serious problem for anyone wishing to attribute a causal role to circumstantial or motivational reasons: an effect must be seen to co-vary with its cause. It would only take one instance of Jack buying flowers for Jill when it was not her birthday or forgetting to buy flowers on her birthday, to threaten the causal link. Similarly, the fact that he loves her prompts him to do various things, including buying her flowers on her birthday. But his not buying her flowers on one birthday would not entail that he did not love her, if he had instead bought her a pear tree.

So among reasons the only serious candidate as a causal influence on action is the teleological. Thus Jack turned on the light in order to check the time: checking the time was the reason for his action. If the time-checking were to be the cause of his turning on of the light, it must be mentally figured while somehow bypassing the causal insufficiency of the intention to turn on the light. When he had turned on the light, Jack performed the action of checking the time. But an intention to check the time would have been causally insufficient for that action. The question is therefore how a teleological reason corresponding to a causally insufficient intention in respect of its own action could be causally sufficient in respect of a prior action.

Our use of the word 'reason' is somewhat inclusive. Any factor that goes towards explaining something can be termed a reason. Clearly not all reasons are cogent enough to be causally efficient. Davidson nominates the type of reason that, from the point of view of the agent, 'rationalizes' his action. This is likely to be a teleological reason but it might also be circumstantial: a person might perform various actions in the weeks before Christmas simply because it was Christmas-time. They would be harder to rationalize at any other time of year. When we try to explain the behaviour of other animals, we might give reasons such as the time of year or the urgency of appetitive desires. We might even cite teleological reasons, for example that birds build nests in order to accommodate their young. But it is clear that these reasons do not rationalize animal behaviour since they are beyond the mental capacity of animals to entertain as *conscious* reasons.

Somehow we have to do justice to the fact that while the wellsprings of human and animal behaviour will be closely related evolutionarily, conscious reasons are in our case decisive. I suggest that rather than causing action they necessitate it via an S-axis. When Jack turns on the light, we know that his reason for doing so will be a necessitating reason since if the objective could be achieved by any other means, the unwanted consequence of Jill's being woken could be avoided. Action is explicable as that which has to take place if the agent's conscious objective is to be realized. If we can realize our objectives with less effort and stress, we tend to do so. Jack's broader aim of catching his flight provides a necessitating reason for a series of actions, each with its own intention. If a reason necessitates an action, which in turn necessitates an intention, the reason will indirectly necessitate the intention. This might help to explain how an idea can occur and be followed quite naturally by appropriate motor behaviour. Reasons are often considered and rejected, or rather *potential* reasons are rejected; they may not be good enough reasons. They should be distinguished from *final* or necessitating reasons.

Suppose that I form an intention to raise my right arm in five minutes' time, for no reason at all, and then do as I intend. Will I thereby have performed an action? In the normal course of events, I would not inexplicably raise my arm: my doing so can only be explained on the assumption that there was an intention, unless I am under hypnosis or my neurology is being externally stimulated. I would claim that whatever necessitates an intention is an action and it seems appropriate to describe my arm-raising as an action. On S-theory the satisfaciend cannot necessitate its condition of satisfaction, so an action cannot necessitate a reason. Just as there could be an intention without an action, there can be an action without a reason.

If the S-model is to be upheld, the necessitating reason, when there is one, must be the action's condition of satisfaction. What exactly is this in the case of the teleological reason? What is the condition of satisfaction of Jack's turning on of the light? If it is the time-checking itself, it constitutes a further action, which can only be the condition of satisfaction of a distinct intention. One way to approach this problem is to imagine that Jack has a 'motivational trajectory', into which are factored his major concerns, such as the wellbeing of his family and the success of his career. The trajectory is more constant than temporary intention but is not rigid. Thanks to a psychological mechanism of some kind, Jack is alerted when his current circumstances bear on his trajectory and require a behavioural response. The mechanism is a development of the evolutionary association that stimulates an animal's response to a particular type of perceptual experience. The animal also has a trajectory, albeit unconscious and centred on survival and reproduction.

In Jack's case the mechanism generates a conscious reason for action (the need for the clock's visibility) and may give it a necessitating force. What his action has to satisfy is the requirement thrown up by the mechanism as a conscious reason. In this sense the reason is the condition of satisfaction of the action. To fulfil the necessitating function, a reason need not be teleological. The fact that tomorrow is Jill's birthday is sufficient to generate a reason for action since she figures prominently among Jack's concerns. He does not need to think about the teleological effect of giving her the flowers. The capacity of conscious reasons to necessitate action illustrates how deeply language has penetrated the human psyche.

Directives and intention

An aspect of intention normally overlooked in philosophy is its evolutionary significance as a coordinating mechanism. In primitive societies there are many occasions when a group needs to organize its behaviour. I am thinking especially of hunting, whose success depends on the transparency with which the future behaviour of individuals with a collective goal can be specified, committed to and relied on. It is essential both that an individual is able to show that he has understood what he is required to do and that he is able to translate this understanding into appropriate behaviour, on pain of being held responsible with reference to his previous commitment. At the same time the activity in question needs to be conceptualized in such a way that the participants can readily construe the goal-oriented significance of their own and others' behaviour. All this is enabled by, and may explain the development of, a special type of intensional language – the language of intention, action and reasons.

How then, in the context of a group activity, is an intention brought into being? The hypothesis I want to defend is that an intention is *in the first instance* the condition of satisfaction of another's directive speech act or imperative. This is the evolutionary origin of the intention. If language evolved from signalling, the intention may have been the first propositional attitude. Like other propositional attitudes, such as the hope, an intention can form spontaneously. Not every intention necessitates a directive. However, every directive has an intention as its condition of satisfaction just as every promise has a hope. As a satisfaciend, an instruction is insufficient to create an intention: the person instructed may choose to ignore it if he objects to it, is physically incapable of obeying it or lacks an incentive to obey it.

Even if an intention is created, it may not lead to an action. But importantly the subject can then be called to account for this failure. To claim that he had formed an intention would be no defence. The evolutionary background is not a liberal democracy in which individuals habitually choose how to act for reasons of their own but a tightly constrained group-dependent struggle for survival where coercion is the norm.

In this light goal-oriented group activity may be characterized in the following way. Just as the knowledge repository has the effect of unifying and streamlining the epistemological stance of the language community, the amenability of behaviour via the intention enables a group to behave as if it were a single organism but with the logistical advantage of numbers. To take the hunting party as an archetype, the contribution of the participants can be consciously controlled as if their motor behaviour were the expression of a single brain. Even without coercion, each participant would be willing to cede autonomy and convert instruction to intention because the pay-off would be so much greater than that of individual endeavour. In a fast-moving situation, instructions are more likely to be issued by a leader than to emerge from a consensus. Once the mechanism is in place, it will be applied more generally: any significant piece of behaviour can be socially scrutinized and subjected to adaptational pressure by being construed as an accountable action. The result may be contrasted with the complex but instinctive activity of social insects such as bees and ants. Language provides both a shortcut to behavioural novelty and imitation and a tool of organization and control.

Taking a cue from Wittgenstein, G. E. M. Anscombe (1957) issued a sceptical challenge, partly to herself. She wanted to establish whether and how the expression of an intention can be distinguished from a prediction about one's own behaviour. The challenge was a way of expressing the problem of the link between intention and behaviour. Intuiting the difference between an intention and a prediction is not the same as explaining it. In my example Jack says 'I am going to wake Jill' on two occasions, once as a prediction and once as the expression of an intention. For Anscombe the problem was exacerbated by the fact (to take my example) that the event – the waking – is the same physical event in both cases. And in both cases Jack seems to know, with equal certainty, that he will wake Jill. So where is the difference? My answer is that it lies in the manner of Jack's conscious meaning, reflected in the intensionality of the verb 'to wake'. Anscombe was working within an analytical tradition that regards intension as something to be explained away rather than embraced. She does not refer to it in her enquiry, which is inconclusive.

At one point she briefly considers whether voluntary action (I would just say 'action') is distinguished by the fact that it can be commanded. She has already proposed that the key to the distinction between intention and prediction is the answer to the question 'Why?' asked of an agent. This will elicit the agent's primary conscious reason for his action, if it is an action, and therefore indirectly his intention. But an agent could also be asked 'Why?' in respect of a piece of meant motor behaviour. The experienced driver could be asked why she changed down and she might reply, 'To go up the hill.' But there need have been no intention. There will, however, have been intension.

If asked why he was about to turn on the light on the two occasions, Jack would reply 'To check the time' and 'To wake Jill.' His prediction on the first occasion ('I am going to wake Jill') is not elicited by the 'Why?' question. However, if a person is commanded to do something and then does it, Anscombe appears to hold that the 'Why?' question fails to distinguish intention from prediction. The person commanded could reply 'You commanded it', but this does not mean that he did it *because* he was commanded to do it. I think Anscombe misses a trick here: the correct reply to the question is surely 'To comply with your command'. The relevance of the 'Why?' question is therefore not at odds with the idea that voluntary action can, distinctively, be commanded.

My similar hypothesis – that any genuine intention could in principle be the condition of satisfaction of a directive speech act

– implies that a piece of behaviour that cannot be produced to order cannot be an action. Is this requirement too sweeping? Involuntary motor behaviour cannot be produced to order – that is what makes it involuntary. It includes sneezing and the shaking that resulted in Alan's dropping of Jim's trophy. Alan could be commanded to shake but his experience would differ from the involuntary shaking experience. On the other hand, meant motor behaviour – the only kind that can underwrite action – can always be commanded. The fact that it is initiated pre-consciously does not prevent its being initiated in response to a directive.

A good test for the hypothesis is winning, which I would claim is never an action. In politics and sport it seems natural for individuals to declare that they intend to win. I have already suggested that in politics this usage is rhetorical since the result of an election is not controllable. But does this apply in sport, when a competitor has a recognized advantage? Sports and games of skill are normally played between roughly equal competitors so that the result is not a foregone conclusion. When it would be, a handicap system is often introduced. So I am prepared to stand by the claim that winning is never an action because, assuming fair play, no one could obey an instruction to win. They could be told they must win, go on to win and be said, in an extensional sense, to have obeyed the instruction, but they would not have obeyed it intensionally. If the final result of an endeavour is beyond the agent's control, he can only be held to account in a limited sense. A football team could be given a dressing down for losing a match, but it would be oppressive for them to be punished. If winning were an action, we would surely need different words for winning by skill and winning by luck.

I next want to consider what is going on when someone intends someone else to do something or that something should happen. For example, Geoffrey intends his son Jeremy to enter the family business. If Jeremy were to do this, would there be any sense in which his action was a condition of satisfaction of his father's intention? It seems that although Jeremy's entering the business is his own action, necessitating his own intention,

Geoffrey can control the result in the negative sense that his say-so is required; the exercise of his say-so would be an intended action on his part. Suppose that he is sensitive to the fact that Jeremy would revolt if he knew that his father 'intended' a career for him. He may not even need to apply pressure if he thinks that the prospect can be made attractive enough. So intending someone to do something need not involve their being aware that this is happening. The result could independently necessitate both intentions as 'dual keys'. Suppose now that Geoffrey owns a racehorse and intends it to run at Newmarket. No intention would be required of the horse, but intended actions would be required of various people under some kind of contractual obligation to Geoffrey.

The point at issue is whether Geoffrey's intentions meet the condition that they could have necessitated directives. If they do not, but stand up as intentions, the hypothesis is flawed. In the case of his racehorse, he clearly could have been instructed to enter it for a certain race at Newmarket. He can in turn simply instruct the relevant people to bring it about that the horse runs. But can the same be said about Jeremy's entering the business? The difficulty here is to find the most appropriate instruction. Possible alternatives are 'Make Jeremy enter the business' and 'Enable Jeremy to enter the business.' Geoffrey would no doubt reply to the first, 'But I can't force Jeremy to act against his will.' He would find himself unable to form an intention to make Jeremy enter the business. He would, on the other hand, have no difficulty in complying with the latter instruction. But it does not seem to capture the force of his intending, unless this is accounted for by two distinct elements: an intention to enable Jeremy to enter the business and a desire that he should enter it. The desire can be as powerful as need be. This analysis would not require dual key intentions since Geoffrey's action would be other than Jeremy's.

A related case, which raises a different problem, is the collective action. Each member of a hunting party could say 'We are going to kill a moose', just as each member of an orchestra could say 'We are going to play the *Eroica*.' The participants each hold an intention but what they are about to do is conceived as a single action. At first sight a single collective action appears to require a single collective intention. What might one of those be? From an empirical perspective there can be nothing over and above the individual intentions of the participants: the last thing the empiricist wants is to have to posit some kind of collective mind. However, when a player says 'We are going to play the *Eroica*', this does not appear to reduce to 'We are each individually going to play our respective parts in the score of the *Eroica*'; neither is he making a mere prediction. In some intuitive sense there is an irreducible collective action, which could follow a single instruction.

On the conventional view, an action stands in some kind of causal relation to an intention, a reason or some other psychological attribute which cannot be shared by more than one person since it is confined to the individual head. On this view there is no way for a set of such individual attributes to acquire collectivity. They could acquire it in the epistemological sense in which we could allow ourselves for the sake of convenience to talk about a collective action. But the philosopher wants precisely to analyze how it is possible to relate individual attributes to talk of collective action and then to decide whether the collective action should, strictly speaking, be decomposed to a set of individual actions. Intentionality will often be invoked in this context. Despite appearances, it is not derived from the word 'intention' but from their common root. Nevertheless, intentions are generally held to exhibit intentionality. Individuals hold intentions whose intentionality is oriented to their individual actions; the only thing that could have intentionality vis-à-vis a collective action would be a collective intention. But the collective intention is inadmissible on empirical grounds. Therefore intentionality entails a decomposition of the collective action.

These difficulties are alleviated by S-theory: the collective action simply necessitates the various individual intentions. To repeat, there is no intentionality. The meant motor behaviour of the individual players does not add up to a collective action, but it is guided by conscious intentions to realize the best possible performance. This is a single conceptual entity, which necessitates the participation of each player in the sense that if any one of them were missing, the performance would suffer. Each player's participation can only be intended; his intention has its condition of satisfaction in the collective action. It is not of the nature of an action that it be performed individually.

There is, however, the question of correlation: can a single condition of satisfaction correlate with multiple satisfaciends? I suggest that since the collective action must have varying representations in the minds of the participants, these are sufficient to allow one-to-one correlation without the action being decomposed. If the collective action is commanded, there is another issue of correlation: each intention would appear to necessitate the same directive. In fact the effective satisfaciend to the individual intention is the auditory percept of the directive in each participant's consciousness.

Institutions, games and rules

Human beings have learnt to base a variety of cooperative models on the amenability of intention. In principle they yield a benefit for each participant greater than the perceived cost. A basic example is the contract, under which two parties undertake to perform non-simultaneous actions reciprocally. The mutual benefit could in principle be achieved through trust; in urban societies, where dealings are typically between strangers, agreement may depend on enforceability. One of the functions of law is therefore to provide an impartial framework within which advantage can be secured by means of cooperation. This gives rise to the paradox that a party to such an agreement can voluntarily enter into it but then have his intentions constrained by it, to the extent that his compliance might appear to be involuntary on the definition offered above. Involuntary action should be defined as excluding that which is knowingly committed to by an agent voluntarily entering a contract.

In other cases individuals formally associate in order to benefit from the achievement of collective goals. Like collective actions, these enterprises depend on the harmonized intentions of individuals. Examples are universities and elected bodies. These institutions qualify as satisfaciends. Their necessitating conditions of satisfaction are complex and somewhat abstract, and participants may have different ideas about them. The community of interest is not always sharply defined and the purpose of the institution may even be contentious. In their methods of internal conflict resolution, institutions often reflect the wider society in microcosm. They resemble shared physical phenotypic extensions in that the activity that sustains them must be normatively focused in specific ways if they are to maintain their credibility and fitness for purpose. Thus the need for internal rules of conduct and procedure. Rules may be formalized to a greater or lesser degree. Over time institutions invariably gather ritual accretions that further regularize behaviour.

The university grew out of the Roman *collegium*, a fraternity or guild with an educational, commercial or ceremonial purpose. The *collegium* was a legal entity, incorporated with a minimum of three persons. It could own property and contract debts; it also offered an opportunity for free association, which was otherwise severely restricted. The burial club was a popular version, owing to a dread of inadequate exequies among the poor. Members contributed during their lives in the knowledge that they would receive a proper funeral. It has been observed that the *collegium* marked a shift in human affairs, after which inheritance would no longer be exclusively genetic. Rather than consisting of the followers of an individual master, as had been the norm in Greece, societies of learning could perpetuate themselves through a genealogy of talent. Developing into universities, by the end of the Middle Ages they had become the official guardians of the knowledge repository and its primary means of transmission.

An analogy can be drawn between the Roman burial club and the modern postal service in that the purpose of each can be expressed as a tangible benefit to individuals. Let's call this type of institution *instrumental*. When I described the postage stamp as a satisfaciend invented to serve a preconceived condition of satisfaction, I could have been referring to the postal system as a whole. In fact assigned function as applied to an object and designated function as applied to an organization are closely related. The university on the other hand is less clearly defined and was not invented but rather evolved under protection. Although it provides some individuals with an education and others with a livelihood, it is also generally reckoned intangibly to benefit society as a whole. This type of institution could be termed *inclusive*. There are also *contractual* institutions, which may be finite or open-ended. The most significant member of this category is probably marriage.

Another institution that traces its origins to the *collegium* is the limited company. It belongs with the bank and the trade union to a group of institutions tied to the market. Commerce could be conducted by solitary individuals but personal liability would prevent the development of more than a rudimentary economy. The limited company allows two groups with potentially conflictive interests – shareholders and managers – to formalize their obligations with a view to mutual advantage without inhibiting its ability to adapt to circumstances. Like a highly evolved organism, it survives or fails in a competitive environment through a process akin to natural selection. One difference is that organisms are not satisfaciends: nothing necessitates you, me or my dog. (This fact, had they but realized it, would have saved Greek ethical philosophers a great deal of fruitless speculation about human purpose.) The company's overriding objective is to be necessitated via demand in the face of competition. Its condition of satisfaction is bound up with the intentional behaviour of its customers, which feeds back to modify its adaptive stance. This is also modified proactively in order to stimulate the intentional behaviour of potential customers.

Another difference from the natural environment is that law serves artificially to reduce hazard, enabling risk to be accurately assessed. It is possible to characterize institutions as quasi-biological self-assembling entities while overlooking the wider context that makes participation attractive. A legally constructed environment is itself the product of intention and has institutional characteristics. The intentions of legislators are influenced by their perceptions of how the laws they enact will influence the future intentions of those affected by them. One means of understanding this complexity is game theory. Legislators factor it when they try to avoid creating conditions in which rational intention leads to undesirable effects.

Wittgenstein introduced the notion that language resembles a game or institution in which meaning is sustained collectively by intentional language use. He offered the analogy of a bank, whose customers know that it relies on their not attempting to withdraw their deposits simultaneously, as they might be tempted to do if they suspected that the bank was in trouble. For the analogy with language to be sustained, there would have to be a parallel between individual action in an institutional context and the intentional making of statements. The former, including the behaviour of a bank's customers, can in principle be explicated by game theory: the individual can ask himself how the institution, from which he benefits, would be affected if everyone else behaved in the same way. It is not clear that such conscientiousness is relevant to the situation in which one person judges how to use words to bring about a state of awareness in another. At that moment most people do not worry excessively about the effect they might be having on the institution of language. In my view language itself is not an institution (in the S-derived sense) since it has no conditions of satisfaction over and above those of speech acts. There is no collective projection of intention beyond the individual intention to communicate in a specific context. The coherence of semantic meaning, even when it shifts, can be explained by the need of individual speakers to be understood.

My approach might be attributed to a free-wheeling Anglo-Saxon disregard. In continental Europe institutions exist for the purpose of protecting languages from abuse and corruption. A francophone might be influenced by the prescriptivism of the

French Academy when making an utterance and feel that in this way he was participating in a collective projection of intention. It is indeed a condition of satisfaction of the Academy that the French language should be preserved in all its magnificence and it has power to impose normativity. But it is not a condition of satisfaction of the French language that it be preserved in an ideal state. A satisfaciend could never have its own existence as a condition of satisfaction.

If language is not an institution, could it be a game? It is difficult to see how, if games were satisfaciends, their conditions of satisfaction could be other than to produce a winner. However, although participants usually try to win, games sometimes end in ties or stalemates without being considered a waste of time. Children's games are often played for their own sake and without a competitive element. There are also solitary games. The psychological appeal of the adult game is deep, both to players and observers. It may have an evolutionary origin in the formal contest between males of the same species, where harm is avoided through animals' (extensional) observance of their own Queensberry Rules. The result could not necessitate the contest since it is indistinguishable from the *status quo* obtaining when no challenger appears. Children's games, like some of their motor behaviour, may originate as a kind of practice for the adult world.

The diversity of games in itself does not count against Wittgenstein's analogy, since it is matched by the way language serves to prime a vast range of typically social contexts, each with its own conventions and expectations. As well as underlining this variety, he compared language in its entirety to a game. If games and language have in common that they are not satisfaciends, it might be possible to view them as pockets of idealized reality, suspended and sustained by means of a public system of convention-like rules. Wittgenstein believed that meaning is constituted by the observance of these rules. When a chess-player moves a piece or a footballer kicks a ball, it makes a difference whether they do so within the context of the game. Outside it this behaviour would have less or no meaning.

A peculiarity of games is that while players engage in meant motor behaviour, spectators perceptually construe. There is no S-axis to cognitive conditions of satisfaction connecting player with player (except insofar as they instruct, encourage or congratulate one another) or player with spectator. When language features in a game, such as a quiz, it functions exactly as it would normally. So the essence of linguistic meaning has no counterpart in the mechanism of the game, where no one *communicates* except as normal. It is therefore difficult see how the game analogy could advance understanding of language. The rules of games can always be made explicit, whereas the rules of language notoriously cannot. Like truth, they are a red herring as far as meaning is concerned.

The status of the extended S-axis

The social character of the collective action and the institution appear to militate against the condition that an S-axis must be confined to the individual organism. I have tried to characterize intention/action as an epistemological, language-dependent development of the basic pattern of meant motor behaviour. This makes it possible to socialize the intention-action axis, both towards the directive with its coordinating function and towards the epistemological reason with its links to the socially conditioned motivational trajectory. At the same time I have tried to explain these relationships by invoking S, which, I have claimed, denotes a form of ontological necessity. The ontological model may have suited the cognitive S-axis to phenomenal and reflective consciousness but the brain's other S-axis threatens to break out of the individual organism. The phenotypic extension creates a similar problem, especially when function is assigned: the condition of satisfaction of the postage stamp presupposes a massive organization planned by human beings but existing independently of them. The question therefore presents itself: are the S-axes between directive, intention, action and reason, or between the stamp and its condition of satisfaction, real or epistemological?

We have already seen how the female phenotypic extension, for example the sundial, does not itself stand as the satisfaciend in an S-axis to the state of awareness of the time of day. Instead the percept of the sundial functions as an internal satisfaciend; the S-axis is confined to the subject's psychology. In the case of perception, the S-axis runs from the brain to the conscious state, with perceptual stimuli taking the role of incorporands. Similarly the auditory percept of the directive is the effective satisfaciend to the intention. The brain supports a complex fusion of S-axes. When a person checks a female extension, its percept is part of the brain's afferent conditions of satisfaction; at the same time the prompted state of awareness is the condition of satisfaction of the percept-as-satisfaciend.

Now when we turn to behaviour, including the manipulation of male phenotypic extensions, we find conditions of satisfaction in the world beyond what an agent alone is able physically to achieve. Cakes are baked, letters are delivered, electricity is generated and ingenious contraptions are landed on the surfaces of other planets. The institution appears to have a life of its own: there may be physical evidence for its existence, including a building displaying its name in big letters. But despite appearances and the participation of perhaps thousands of people, the institution's S-axis to its condition of satisfaction remains psychologically modelled and controlled. The systems responsible for the delivery of letters and the generation of electricity are psychologically modelled and controlled. This entails that ultimately they are projected by individuals, acting in association in the light of their psychological representations of advantage and of the relevant intentions of others. The systems depend on inorganic materials but they *work* on the model of biological function, with meaning as the indispensable organizing principle.

My radically internalist claim is that S-axes involving the brain are no less confined to the organism than those between genotype and phenotype. So are they real or epistemological? I would say that they illustrate the falsity of the antithesis. Organisms consist of S-axes: that *is* their ontology. Physical components are not organized into S-axes like the parts of a machine. Above a certain level of organization, there is in biological systems no reality independent of S-axes; they are served by lower levels of organization that may turn out to conceal further S-axes. The examples of intention and action, of assigned function and the institution reveal that our epistemology – how we conceptualize, model and manipulate our external world – also conforms to S-axes. Because our epistemology is rooted in the ontology of the brain, it cannot but conform. The real basis of behaviour is neurology in S-axes; the basis of our understanding of behaviour and what it can achieve is also figured in S-axes. There are no grounds for a qualitative, Cartesian separation of biological ontology from epistemology or of the brain from the conscious states it supports. The essence of epistemology is meaning, which on S-theory becomes ontological.

Science and epistemology

Evolutionary internalism, as I would term my position, follows the empiricist tradition in casting doubt on our ability to acquire knowledge of the external world that is not coloured by the means by which it is acquired. The evolutionary component is a recognition that the channels of assimilation will have been adapted to purpose by selective pressure and therefore express a history of comparative success in dealing with the external world. They will have become reliable. When philosophers investigate the reliability of our channels of assimilation, the discussion turns on the question of certainty. A form of knowledge commonly cited as a benchmark is scientific knowledge, which is underpinned by natural laws apparently independent of our mental construction and indeed prevailing prior to any form of life. This assumption was challenged by Thomas Kuhn (1962), who argued that scientific observation is theory-dependent. That is, like ordinary perception it is inevitably construed with reference to existing patterns of assimilation. In science existing patterns constitute what Kuhn famously termed a *paradigm*. A paradigm may reign unchallenged for centuries while the majority of scientists work within its terms of reference. Even when anomalous data appear, perhaps with the invention of more precise instruments, it will first be assumed that they can be made to fit the paradigm. Eventually pressure will build but, even when critical, will not itself force a paradigm shift: that requires the articulation of a new theory better able to explain enough of the facts. The new paradigm thus arrives with its own techniques for the construal of evidence and for dealing with the new anomalies that will inevitably appear. Like military victors, its proponents will be able to write the history of the shift and lend it an aura of inevitability.

The history of astronomy provided Kuhn with an unfolding case study. Although a heliocentric system was proposed by Aristarchus in the third century BC, like Democritus' atomism it was not based on sufficiently compelling evidence. Instead the geocentric Ptolemaic system became the dominant model in antiquity, although it was never able to accommodate every observation of planetary motion. Discrepancies were dealt with by small adjustments, for example to Ptolemy's system of compounded circles. The result over time was a massive increase in complexity, which by the sixteenth century had begun to seem too high a price to pay for dubious accuracy. Because the Ptolemaic system could not solve its own problems, the situation addressed by Copernicus could be described as an intellectual crisis, compounded by the urgent question of the length of the calendar year. In fact his heliocentric theory made slow progress for a century since, although simpler, it was no more accurate than Ptolemy's. It was only when Kepler produced his laws of planetary motion that astronomers were decisively converted. Newton subsequently produced his more universal laws of motion and gravitational attraction, from which he was able mathematically to deduce Kepler's laws. However he did not attempt to model the effects of gravity when more than two bodies are in play, a common enough scenario in celestial mechanics. This deficiency stimulated an enormous mathematical effort in the eighteenth and nineteenth centuries, but certain phenomena, notably an oddity in the orbit of Mercury at its closest point to the Sun, were explained only by Einstein's general theory of relativity.

Kuhn cites an experiment by J. S. Bruner and Leo Postman, which is worth mentioning parenthetically because it illustrates how cognitive confidence is linked to affect. Subjects were asked to identify a series of playing cards, some of which had been made to show, for example, red spades or black hearts. They only became aware of these anomalies when their assumption that they were seeing ordinary cards could no longer be sustained, in other words on surprisingly prolonged exposure. After they had correctly identified two or three of the anomalous cards, they had little difficulty. A few failed to identify the anomalous cards at all and showed signs of distress. Postman told Kuhn that even when setting up the experiment he found looking at the anomalous cards acutely uncomfortable. This affective dimension may help to explain why paradigms are not easily dislodged. The implications of a paradigm shift may be felt in the wider culture, where resistance may be articulated in non-scientific terms.

Kuhn discovered that he was poking at a hornet's nest. Many (rightly) considered that he was challenging the objectivity of science. He was (wrongly) accused of relativism and of questioning the idea of scientific progress. He had a famous run-in with Karl Popper, who was haunted by the manipulation of science in totalitarian societies and believed that the independence of scientific enquiry was connected to its claims to objectivity, supported by the principle of falsifiability. Kuhn acknowledged the influence of Wittgenstein but this did little to assuage those philosophers who for various reasons felt it necessary to defend science. The truth is that Wittgenstein has never been flavour of the month in the United States, where the controversy was largely played out. Putnam and Kripke took Kuhn seriously enough to respond by developing 'essentialist' positions under which the scientifically accessible reality of the external world would determine conceptual categories rather than vice versa. With Kripke, water would necessarily be H_2O; with Putnam, the meaning of 'water' would be determined by the substance's microstructure, unmediated by prevailing scientific theory. The discovery that water is H_2O could therefore be taken objectively to be an advance.

Kuhn would later (1990) reply that the meanings of terms like 'water' and 'mass' are embedded within a particular paradigmatic view. Each paradigm has its own taxonomy of natural kinds. When the meaning of a natural kind term is adjusted, the whole system is affected. Not only will a natural kind term vary in meaning from one paradigm to another, it may not be strictly translatable. Nothing could evoke in us the associations attaching to the ancient Greek use of the word for water. The same applies to conceptual terms. Einstein gave a meaning to the word 'mass' that could not be captured on Newtonian assumptions: to understand 'mass' in Einstein's sense, one needs to be acquainted with his theory. Cultures may therefore hold mutually incommensurable concepts just as individuals wield non-convergent intensions. Despite Kuhn's satisfying swipe at the twin-headed Hydra, Putnamian natural kind externalism and Kripkean rigid designation, for which he was in a sense responsible, live on.

There is a tension in science between explanation and description. In order to explain, science leans towards simplicity and universality. But it must always remain grounded in observation, which is likely to throw up exceptions to the prevailing explanatory theory, especially when technology is undergoing change. The path taken by science is determined by how these contradictions are resolved. Kuhn's contribution was to suggest that observation cannot fulfil the role conventionally expected of it, namely to limit any theory with the same external, neutral point of reference or criterion of truth. Because his anti-referentialist stance accords well with S-theory, it is tempting to lend it an evolutionary perspective as a means of deflecting the charge of relativism to which S-theory is also exposed. Thus the development and application of scientific methodology can be construed as a special case of cognitive adaptation, which also reveals a balance between consolidation and responsiveness, mediated by plasticity. Perceptual parsing and construal could have been streamlined by being reduced to simple templates, but at the cost of rendering the organism ill-equipped to deal with novelty. In this light scientific progress can be seen as a variety of evolutionary progress. In both cases the term is contentious because it implies an external criterion of perfection. Like Kuhn, however, one might not wish to deny that progress is a meaningful concept. We are after all talking about cognitive adaptation. Suppose that evolution had left an organism highly adapted to a certain environment by virtue of a phenotypic character but less capable of adjusting to catastrophic change than it would have been had the character been less developed. The claim to progress would ring hollow. But what kind of environmental change could render a cognitive adaptation a liability? Presumably one in which the basis of *a priori* judgments was undermined, so that, for example, things did just disappear or looked bigger instead of smaller when they were further away. In other words the term 'progress' is as valid in the scientific domain as the working assumption that the external world presents a structural consistency, however it may be theorized, through time and space.

Science seeks to capture this structural consistency in laws of nature. But do laws of nature describe ontological consistency? Did they exist before they were formulated? Or are they no more than empirical generalizations to which there happen to be no exceptions? As an aid, this is what Newton's laws look like:

(1) A body remains at rest, or moves in a straight line at a constant speed, unless acted upon by an outside force.
(2) Acceleration of a body is proportional to the outside force acting on it.
(3) When one body exerts a force on a second body, the second body exerts an equal and opposite force on the first body.
(4) Two bodies attract each other with a force (gravity) that is directly proportional to the mass of each body and inversely proportional to the square of the distance between them.

The epistemological interpretation of laws of nature is supported by the fact that they are invariably shown to be provisional by further advances in knowledge. However, the exceptionless generalization somehow fails to do justice to our sense that a law does not *admit* exceptions. In other words laws have, or can be given, a modal force: Newton's first law could be expressed as 'A body *must* remain at rest...' This is related to the modality in 'There must be three apples in that bag', where the speaker implies that he has strong grounds for a belief, which are transferable to the hearer. Newton had general empirical grounds for his laws, transferable in principle to any interested party via the knowledge repository. A scientist in possession of a law will in general be more empowered than a scientist in possession of an exceptionless generalization, just as a person who has been told 'There must be three apples in that bag' may be at an advantage over a person who has been told 'There are three apples in that bag'. The moment a law of nature ceases to empower is the moment it ceases to be a law of nature.

For similar reasons, causal relations have generally been taken to be lawlike and therefore necessary. When we engage in meant motor behaviour, it is normally with the aim of becoming causally relevant. If our behaviour is to have point, we inevitably factor causation as it applies to the circumstances we want to affect. The confidence that a certain effect will or must follow when causally sufficient conditions obtain empowers us both to predict and to interact with the external world. If a pot of water is placed over a fire, the expectation that the water will heat up is invariably justified. No benefit could be derived from a more fastidious view of causal relations as non-lawlike conjunctions; our empowerment would be compromised for no good reason. The causal principle is like an accessible law of nature: we do not need to be scientists or have special equipment to believe we witness its operation. Because the principle seems so reliable and immediate, our belief in causation has become entangled with our perceptual construal of the way in which objects behave, with or without our intervention. But the parameters of perceptual construal are *a priori*, whereas laws of nature are *a posteriori*: they are open to rejection on empirical grounds. By testing them, we may learn something about the world. In a contrary manner we have somehow got ourselves into the position where causality – the lawlike causal principle – is not falsifiable by experience. If, given the presence of a cause, its expected effect does not follow, we assume the presence of some further, causally relevant factor.

There is no barrier to the further assumption that any observable state or event has a causal explanation, even when it could never be repeated. If we were dealing with a law of nature, we would insist on proper testing. But nothing could count for us as a falsifying test of causality. If modality can attach itself to an *a posteriori* law (a body *must* remain at rest ...), so much more readily will it attach itself to an *a priori* lawlike relation between a cause and its effect. The position that every state or event has a causal explanation thus effortlessly mutates into *determinism*, according to which effects necessarily follow their causes and no state or event *could* have occurred differently. Unfalsifiable determinism is orthodoxy among contemporary philosophers, psychologists and neuroscientists.

Causation and science

Discussions of causation often acknowledge the seminality of Hume. He was the first to notice that because causes are distinct from their effects and contain nothing from which their effects could be deduced, we must rely on a form of inference when we attribute lawlike powers to them.

> Our idea of necessity and causation arises entirely from the uniformity, observable in the operations of nature; where similar objects are constantly conjoined together, and the mind is determined by custom to infer the one from the appearance of the other. These two circumstances form the whole of that necessity, which we ascribe to matter. Beyond the constant *conjunction* of similar bodies, and the consequent *inference* from one to the other, we have no notion of any necessity, or connexion. (EHU 8.1.5)

Thus equipped, we can formulate laws and make predictions about the external world, that is, science can carry on. But we could never have access to what really goes on out there as distinct from the ideas formed by our observations. One such idea is that of causal necessity.

Hume's case was salutary in his own time and is still influential. But it conceals problems of interpretation. In the same passage in the *Enquiry* he could say:

> It is universally allowed, that matter, in all its operations, is actuated by a necessary force, and that every natural effect is so precisely determined by the energy of its cause, that no other effect, in such particular circumstances, could possibly have resulted from it. (8.1.4)

This is as clear a statement of determinism as one could wish for. When Hume says 'it is universally allowed', he could mean 'it is universally believed', tacitly distancing himself from a belief unwarranted on the principles he has laid out. On the other hand the determinist claim is central to his argument at this point; he never qualifies it, except by implication of his scepticism. But if he was a determinist, he will have held a belief that he believed he could not justify.

Some commentators (Wright, 1983) have argued that Hume was a 'sceptical realist', combining scepticism about the capacity of the mind to grasp unmediated reality with a certain belief about the nature of that reality, namely that it is subject to a type of causal necessity. For Hume science will have tended to reinforce such a belief, while being conducted on empirical principles and therefore consistently with his scepticism.

The cultural background is relevant. Hume was aware that his readership contained two broad groups: those who believed in supernatural causation and those who believed in scientific causation. In fact determinism was far from universally allowed: many people believed (and still believe) that God can intervene in natural processes in the sense that he can break laws of nature. These groups were engaged in the same long culture war that was to surround Darwinism. Although his sceptical argument was directed against supernaturalism, Hume cannot have been comfortable with the fact that, by challenging the objectivity of laws of nature, it also undermined the claims of naturalism. He could not have known that the scientific view would eventually become orthodoxy (or that this would not mean the end of supernaturalism). If he could not provide a knockdown argument against supernaturalism, he could at least avoid levelling the playing-field and indeed contributing to the defeat of naturalism. For this reason he may have allowed himself to introduce a bias that was strictly unwarranted on his terms. If he was a realist, he might have felt justified in doing so. I merely conclude that, although Hume thought as deeply as anyone about causal necessity, nothing in his work compels acceptance of it.

Despite his ambiguities, Hume succeeded in casting the problem of causation in a way that has not been superseded. In short, nothing subsequently revealed by science has settled the metaphysical issue. The regularities of nature overwhelmingly indicate the existence of some form of metaphysical necessity but scientific observation is still bounded by epistemology, in no sense to its own detriment. Philosophers however are left with the perennial problem of how to make progress in metaphysics in any way comparable with the advance of science.

In order to appreciate the difficulty, let's take the scenario of a boy, by the name of Billy, throwing stones at a bottle. One of the stones finally smashes it. We would naturally say that the smashing of the bottle has been caused. But by what? Possible causes are: Billy, Billy's throw, the accuracy of the throw, the stone, the combined weight and velocity of the stone, the impact of the stone, the microstructure of the stone combined with its velocity, Billy's brain, Billy's motor behaviour, Billy's intention or even some experience of Billy's earlier in the day. An obvious choice would be the stone. But how can a mere stone be the cause of the smashing? What differentiates it from the other stones that Billy could have selected? Presumably its being thrown. But if it had been smaller or thrown with less force, it might not have smashed the bottle. So in the stone of a certain size, thrown with a certain force, we have a primitive fact. And we can see that the most plausible candidates for the cause of the smashing are 'causal facts'; the more complex a fact is allowed to become, the better able it is to capture what is causally relevant in a given situation. I would also say that the more complex a fact is allowed to become, the more clearly is it an externalization of a language-enabled psychological state.

Russell (1913) took the radical step of proposing that causation be eliminated from philosophical discourse as 'a relic of a bygone age'. He pointed out that, although it seems scientific to philosophers, science itself ignores it in practice. As Newton's illustrate, the laws of an established science do not refer to it. Russell observed that 'in the motions of mutually gravitating bodies, there is nothing that can be called a cause, and nothing that can be called an effect; there is merely a formula.' For the purpose of a law, a body can simply be said to 'act on' another. No cause need be specified. Laws reveal constancies within a given physical system which can be expressed by means of differential equations and which allow predictions to be made about the behaviour of the system or its constituents. Causality by contrast extrapolates to the entire physical universe from construed phenomena. Causation is also time-directional: we would question the notion that an effect could precede its cause. By contrast, although they manifest themselves in time-directional processes, the constancies revealed by scientific laws are not asymmetrical in this sense: they serve equally to determine past states of the system from present states.

Russell's paper appeared shortly after Einstein had explained the curvature of space-time and several years before the emergence of quantum theory, which describes a level of physical reality where prediction can only be made within bounds of probability. If laws operate at this level, it is generally accepted that they must be probabilistic laws. This in itself has not been fatal to causality since causing can, it seems, be redefined as 'making more likely'. Nevertheless quantum indeterminacy might have been expected to tell against determinism. Philosophical arguments along these lines have not found favour. When Einstein observed that 'God does not play with dice', he was refusing to accept that quantum theory need be the last word on ontology. There could yet be a deeper level of reality that was deterministic or there could be a 'hidden variable' whose existence would complete quantum theory and render it deterministic. Quantum indeterminacy is connected to the anomaly whereby observation affects what is being observed. We would need to understand the phenomenon better before making it the basis of a metaphysical position. Similarly, we cannot infer from its complexity that chaos in any of its forms is non-deterministic.

Nevertheless one might wonder, with Russell, why causation has not been eliminated from philosophy. Jonathan Schaffer (2007) has this to say:

> Causation, according to various contemporary philosophers, is required for the analysis of metaphysical concepts such as persistence, scientific concepts such as explanation and disposition, epistemic concepts such as perception and warrant, ethical concepts such as action and responsibility, mental concepts such as functional role and conceptual content, and linguistic concepts such as reference. Elimination is not just unjustified; it would be catastrophic.

This is only half the picture: the topics listed by Schaffer have in common that they are unresolved. Might this by any chance have to do with the fact that they implicate causation? After all, no defensible philosophical theory has ever rested on it. Analytic philosophy is in danger of resembling a failing Kuhnian paradigm, with causation cast in the role of geocentricity. The catastrophe should perhaps be welcomed.

Counterfactual dependence

Even if our understanding of causation is bounded by epistemology, philosophers will always want to follow Hume's example and deepen it by analyzing the concept. One of the more promising strategies rests on *counterfactual dependence*. Event B is counterfactually dependent on event A if is the case that, were it not for A, B would not have occurred. Thus the striking of a match causes it to light since the lighting is counterfactually dependent on, or would not have occurred without, the striking. But the lighting is also counterfactually dependent on the presence of oxygen and the dryness of the match. We might not want to say that the presence of oxygen is a cause of the lighting. We might instead want to describe it as a contributory condition. If a smoker contracted lung cancer, we might say that his smoking caused his lung cancer. But his lung cancer is also counterfactually dependent on his having lungs, and indeed on his being alive, neither of which would we class as causes. Unfortunately it has proved impossible to find a criterion, applicable across cases, with which to divide relevant factors into causes and contributory conditions. Suppose that a scientific experiment was being conducted in conditions that specifically excluded oxygen but that, owing to a malfunction, air was allowed in. If, as a result, the experiment went wrong, the presence of oxygen would likely be regarded as a cause. How does the presence of oxygen in this case differ from its presence when the match is struck?

Another problem for counterfactual dependence is 'preemption'. In a famous thought experiment, Suzy joins her friend Billy in throwing stones at a bottle. Suzy's stone arrives first and smashes it. Billy's stone lands in such a way that, had the bottle not already been smashed, it would have smashed it. Therefore, although we would naturally say that Suzy's throw is the cause of the smashing, the smashing is not counterfactually dependent on her throw: had she not thrown, the bottle would still have been smashed. Indeed, if Billy was on his own and had decided to keep throwing stones until he had smashed the bottle, the smashing would arguably not be counterfactually dependent on the throw that caused it. In this case, we might want to follow Hume and add a further criterion, namely that of contiguity: it is Suzy's stone that makes contact with the bottle.

There is also the question of overdetermination. Suppose that A and B simultaneously fire their guns at C and C dies, hit in the head by A and in the chest by B. Presumably there is a cause of death. But C's death is not counterfactually dependent on any one thing. If either A or B had not fired, he would still have died.

We might want to say that A and B's shots jointly caused C's death. But it cannot be counterfactually dependent on the combination, since it would have occurred if either shot had not been fired. There are various ways of buttressing counterfactual dependence, but the more complicated the analysis, the less plausible it becomes as a basis of intuition. A possibility that must be considered is that the concept of causation simply cannot be analyzed, that when we talk of causes we abstract from situations immediately to the concept. An important area where this could present a practical problem is the law, since causation by individuals is relevant to their legal responsibility. If the concept of causation cannot be analyzed, legal theory would be dependent on its subjective interpretation, leading potentially to inconsistency. The difficulty of finding a criterion for causation is compounded by the requirement that justice should be seen to be done. Counterfactual dependence has provided the so-called 'but-for' test, whereby a person is responsible for some harm if, but for his action, it would not have occurred. This test has to be supplemented since otherwise in the example above A and B would both be acquitted of C's murder. Greater difficulties affect tort law, which can be used to recover damages from a person found liable for an injury. Here responsibility often needs to be limited. In Leonard Hoffman's example, a man consulted his doctor about a bad knee before a mountaineering trip. But for the doctor's advice that he should not worry, he would have pulled out. During the trip he is injured by a rock fall, which has nothing to do with his knee. A principle is required which absolves the doctor of responsibility for the injury. When such a principle is found, it will allow us to say that the doctor did not cause the injury, rather than that he caused it without being responsible for it. This suggests that the concept of causation in law is guided by the concept of responsibility rather than vice versa. This is reminiscent of the way in which we attribute responsibility to an agent by using the word 'intentional' to describe an unintended consequence.

Downward metaphysical necessity

When I became aware of the pervasive presence of S in biological systems, I had no reason to doubt that non-biological ontology was causal, although I was averse to determinism. The lawlike behaviour of the universe makes it highly likely that there is some kind of metaphysical necessity; otherwise its lawlikeness would be unexplained. Causal necessity has appeared to be the only candidate. Objections to determinism normally appeal to randomness, for example at the quantum level, rather than to an alternative type of necessity. Because S indicated the presence of an alternative type of necessity, at first I suspected that biological systems might have their own form of ontology. But this notion was simply too bizarre. Although organisms are discrete, they interact seamlessly with their environments. It was more likely that non-biological ontology had been misconceived. If the necessitation of the S-axis was real, could it therefore have implications for metaphysics in general?

Bear in mind that metaphysical necessity could never be observed, as Hume pointed out. Science therefore cannot rule on the matter, although it may be able to help us. At a certain level the universe has been found to consist of particles in fields of force. When particles such as atoms are penetrated, they are found to consist of smaller particles in fields of force until the quantum level is reached and the distinction between particles and forces is submerged in the wave function. There are four forces: gravity, electro-magnetism and the strong and weak nuclear forces. How is causal necessity supposed to operate at the level of particles and forces? A possible answer is that particles bounce off one another in a chain reaction that manifests linear causal necessity. But how could forces be made to fit into this picture? When particles are deconstructed to smaller particles and forces, does the necessity of their causal interactions persist? A second problem is the role of microstructure in constitutive or emergent causation. The malleability of a lump of gold is a natural phenomenon requiring explanation: it is attributed to properties of its molecular structure, which somehow cause the malleability. The arrangement of H_2O molecules determines whether water is liquid or forms ice.

I hope I have persuaded you that, although the colloquial use of causation is very convenient and entirely permissible, it is a deeply suspect concept from any analytical perspective. There is no systematic way to exclude epistemology from the picture: the association of necessitating force with entities bound and parsed in perception, which survives only until they are taken apart by science, is unsustainable. But, as Russell pointed out, the picture is not scientific: physicists do not ask themselves how particles or forces can have causal efficacy. By relegating causation to epistemology, we can clear the ground for a more plausible general theory of necessity, entirely consistent with the findings of science. I propose that metaphysical necessity, which constitutes the 'glue of the universe', runs downward rather than upward. The deconstruction of matter to its fundamental components can never expose downward metaphysical necessity (DMN) to view. It is conducted by the four forces but is not to be identified with them: they may also eventually be deconstructed or unified. But no assumption need be made in respect of the ultimate constitution of matter. The fact that a physical state, such as chaos or quantum indeterminacy, is unamenable to laws has no implication for the presence of DMN. Unlike causality, it cannot be called into question by empirical evidence. The higher-level properties of materials, such as the malleability of a lump of gold, necessitate downwards to their microstructure, which necessitates as far as the fundamental physical level, whatever that may be. The goal of a unified physical theory may only be achievable at the metaphysical level (I am not qualified to pronounce on this). Since the ontological S-axis is peculiar to biological systems, the unification of physics and biology might also depend on metaphysics.

DMN can therefore be substituted for upward constitutive or emergent causation without loss of explanatory power, and quite possibly with an increase. Take the issue of laws of nature. All observable events, including those which have not been brought under laws of nature, reflect ontological necessity (= DMN), as did the universe before the arrival of life. Lawlikeness is therefore universal owing to the underlying presence of DMN, which can be said to *constrain* physics. I would hazard that mathematics is a form of constraint and another manifestation of DMN. Laws are a conceptualization of lawlikeness and for that reason are essentially epistemological. However, they are more than exceptionless generalizations since they describe a physical reality that is ontologically constrained from permitting exceptions. The physical manner of constraint will always be a matter for further scientific discovery. Laws are therefore *a posteriori*.

Our attraction to causality is perfectly reasonable. Given our interactive point of view, it is the most practical way of representing the universal force of DMN. It never lets us down. It is just that there is no causal necessity, as Miss Anscombe (1971) almost alone among philosophers intuited, even though she failed to make a convincing case. This would be a tall order since the argument cannot appeal to facts; the case for determinism will tend to prevail by appearing to be *a posteriori* or fact-driven, while depending illicitly on the force of *a priori* judgment.

This *a posteriori* character in fact betrays the principal weakness of causation as a vehicle of necessity: it is insufficiently abstract. Firstly, there are several types of cause. Aristotle named four. I have tried to limit reference to the linear and constitutive types. If these could be reduced to a single type, the case for a unitary causal necessity would be strengthened. But their construed roles are radically heterogeneous.

The virtue of abstraction is evident in the remarkable case of the uranium-238 atom. This radioactive substance was synthesized at least 6 billion years ago and has a half-life of 4.5 billion years – half of its remaining atoms decay over that period. The decay event is not caused by an external factor and no theory can predict when a given atom will decay – indeed it is impossible to distinguish between them. Take an atom decaying today. If the decay event is caused in a linear sense, the causal train will have to have been set in motion 6 billion years ago inside the atom when it was formed.

On the premise of DMN, the position might be described as follows. The uranium-238 atom is suspended in a certain state for 6 billion years by a balance of forces: the balance is metaphysically necessitated by the integrity of the atom. The balance is not static: there is a constant movement of particles and shifting of forces inside the atom. But at a certain point the configuration of particles and forces is such that the balance is upset, triggering the decay event. By virtue of the atom's size and the nature of its particles and forces, there is a statistical probability of 50% that the fatal configuration will occur in the course of 4.5 billion years.

This case is of interest partly because the causal model has to admit an intersection of the linear and constitutive types of causation. There is no explanation on the causal model for the failure of constitutive causation except as an event caused in a linear fashion. The decay event must therefore be treated as the effect of a linear causal train. There is no problem of explanation when an external causal train hits an object and destroys it. The problem in this case is that the internal train has components which must simultaneously be part of the atom's constitutive causation. This kind of difficulty is simply avoided by the adoption of DMN, largely because it has no requirement for sufficiency. Upward causation must rest on lower-level causal sufficiency vis-à-vis higher-level properties. There is nowhere this sufficiency could come from. If it were thought to pertain to a conjunction of some kind at the lower level, it would have to be shown how the conjunction differed from the emergent property supposedly caused by it. The absence of causal sufficiency is of course exploited by the biological S-axis.

On one particular issue physics is compelled to admit the concept of causation in its search for a solution: the origin of the universe. That is to say, the problem can only be framed as the problem of how an event can lack a cause. Could it be conceptualized more satisfactorily with reference to DMN? The position might be cast as follows. As soon as the universe comes into existence with the Big Bang, DMN is present. It precedes the formation of matter and the differentiation of forces but it becomes their organizing principle as the universe expands and cools. At the point of origin, the universe can perhaps be imagined as a non-necessitating, or self-necessitating, singularity, outside time, without any physical characteristics that we could understand and indeed beyond the distinction between physics and metaphysics. For some reason the singularity is not self-sustaining: DMN represents the fall-out from its catastrophic failure, a nostalgic echo of its organizing principle.

Because it is so elusive, I have had difficulty in conveying the precise nature of S-necessitation. I have probably been guilty of covertly invoking counterfactuality, especially in the notion that a phenotypic extension is necessitated by its condition of satisfaction. You may have taken me to imply, for example, that the trapping of flies is counterfactually dependent on the spider's web – that the trapping cannot occur without the web. It is important that S-necessitation, and by implication DMN, be purged of counterfactuality, which, like laws of nature, is epistemological. It may be the case that the fly-trapping is counterfactually dependent on the web, but this is only a reflection of underlying constraint. In the area of behaviour, it frequently happens that a condition of satisfaction necessitates a satisfaciend without being counterfactually dependent on it. Suppose for example that the orchestra that performs the *Eroica* can call on stand-in players for all the parts. It would not be true to say that the performance as a collective action is counterfactually dependent on the intentions of the regular players, since, if they had all been indisposed, it could have gone ahead. To take an even clearer example, propositional attitudes are often not counterfactually dependent on their speech act satisfaciends: a person can spontaneously form an intention or a hope. S-necessitation instead describes the relation between the caught fly and the web, between the actual action and the intentions of those whose action it is, or between a promise-induced hope and the corresponding promise. The conceptual possibility of an alternative satisfaciend, or of the absence of a satisfaciend, has no bearing on these necessary relations.

Freedom of action

And so we arrive at the question of free will. If determinism were true, it would be a paradox worth investigating that most of us feel our actions are freely chosen. I say 'most of us' in deference to the psychologist Susan Blackmore, who when looking at a menu says to herself, 'I wonder what she'll choose?' Either one will find reductive explanations of our sense of freedom plausible or one will sympathize with Samuel Johnson. When he exclaimed, 'Sir, we *know* our will is free, and there's an end on it', he was venting exasperation at the tendency of theory to ignore the evidence of experience. He was exposed to a double whammy: the new scientific determinism that so impressed Hume (his junior by 18 months) mirrored the Protestant doctrine of predestination. If God is omniscient, he must know the future, including how we will act. Therefore, since it is knowable, how we will act must already be in some way determined. However, this undermines the notion that an action can be good or evil as well as introducing the further problem of how God could have created a world where he foresaw evil without being responsible for it.

Just as medieval thinkers wrestled with such imponderables, later philosophers who have wished to retain free will have struggled to reconcile it with determinism in a general approach, going back to Hume, known as *compatibilism*. One compatibilist argument runs roughly as follows. When Tim goes into a sweetshop, his choice is limited by how much money he has on him, by his taste in sweets and by his concern for his health. Within these parameters he has a range of genuine options. Nevertheless his final choice will be causally determined, although of course he may not realize it. His free will consists in his circumscribed freedom of choice, including the freedom to walk out empty-handed.

I *think* by 'free will' I am referring to something else – something more qualitative and psychological. Better off people don't have more of it. But I am going to steer clear of the compatibilist debate because I believe that determinism can be refuted and therefore does not need to be rendered compatible. Instead I want to return to the theory of action already propounded, in case it can throw light on our notion of free will. None of what follows is intended as an argument against determinism: the case, such as it is, has already been made.

Tim is trying to decide whether to go into the office or to work from home. If he goes to the office, he will be able to look at his post and run over the new project with his assistant; if he stays at home, he will get more done and will avoid sitting in his car for two hours. How does he finally decide? On the present theory, his behaviour is amenable to conscious reasons, which are able to necessitate action. Tim may line up the two sets of reasons and feel that he is weighing them in a balance. Reasons may combine in such a way that their joint force is decisive. They may also be reinforced by desires of which the agent is conscious or unconscious. Tim enjoys being at home because the coffee is better and he can have lunch with his wife, considerations that may well tip the balance. Tim may be deluding himself in thinking that he can get more done at home; his 'reasons' for staying at home may disguise desires. However, if we try to reduce all his reasons to desires, we face the problem that no explanation is available for the conversion of simple desire to behaviour, whereas there would appear to be an explanation for the conversion of a reason to an action. An appetitive desire can powerfully propel a person towards behaving in a way appropriate to its satisfaction, but it could never achieve the final necessitating force and focus of a conscious reason. A non-appetitive desire, such as the desire for a new mobile phone, will often prompt a justifying reason, as it were to do its work for it.

Having evolved as social beings, we are sensitive to normative influences on our behaviour, which come into play when the interests of other people are affected. Suppose that Tim remembers that he has arranged to play squash with a colleague at lunchtime; by staying at home, he would let this person down.

For some people the obligation to honour a commitment counts more strongly than for others. For some people such an obligation would constitute a necessitating reason. Tim feels torn between his sense of obligation and his growing desire to stay at home. He can feel the necessitating force of the obligation, which seems to overshadow the other reasons he has carefully lined up. At this point his will becomes relevant. Rather than describing a faculty that he can switch on, it is a way of conceptualizing the feeling of necessitation by a conscious normative reason in conflict with a non-normative impulse. Strength of will denotes a capacity for one's actions to be necessitated by such reasons. This capacity is connected to the manner in which a person represents his reasons to himself; he may consciously have cultivated a particular mode of representation. A person could also set himself a normative goal with little or no relevance to the interests of others, for example by going on a diet. If Tim decided to avoid eating sweets, there would be moments during the day when his will was sorely tested. In order to overcome the temptation, he would probably remind himself why losing weight is a good idea.

This interpretation of action and will in my view makes it more coherent to speak of 'freedom of action'. Arguments against free will are often based on the findings of Libet and others in respect of the pre-conscious initiation of motor behaviour. A clear distinction between motor behaviour and action shows this evidence to be beside the point: we would be handicapped – practically paralyzed – by a 'freedom of motor behaviour' that required it to be consciously initiated. The pertinent question concerning freedom of action is whether a subject's sense of autonomy in a psychological conflict involving one or more conscious reasons is justified. A determinist would hold that the outcome follows of necessity from the causal interaction of external stimuli and internal predispositions. Conscious reasons do not fit within the causal model and therefore cannot be found a role. If determinism were true, the sense of autonomy would be unjustified and might be explained as an evolutionary trait which made us more likely to behave in a certain way. But if determinism is false and conscious reasons do have a role, the burden of proof will fall on the sceptic, to show why the sense of autonomy is an illusion. I repeat a point made earlier, that if organisms were satisfaciends, their psychological states might well be necessitated. Instead a subject has at least some freedom in the way she represents her reasons to herself. The individual's motivational trajectory is also highly relevant to the production of conscious reasons. When it shifts, for example when a person decides to give up investment banking in order to become a school teacher, it normally does so under the influence of conscious experience and reflection.

Biological deconstraint

In addition to the acceptance of determinism, a notable feature of the contemporary intellectual landscape is the belief that all behaviour is at root self-interested. That is, behaviour that might appear to be altruistic can be explained in principle as in some way benefiting the agent, despite appearing to incur a cost. This view has been around for a long time, for most of which it has been in conflict with a religious ideal. It received a fresh twist in the mid-twentieth century, when evolutionary biology was synthesized with genetics. With this development the heritability of fitness could for the first time be adequately addressed. It also opened up new territory to causal explanation since genes could be argued to determine behaviour, in which case they would naturally be geared to promoting the interests of their owners. Environmental factors would form part of the explanation but would be subject to deterministic influences of their own.

Richard Dawkins (1976) has been prominent in championing the gene as the unit of evolutionary selection. Before the 1960s evolution had been thought to involve competition between individuals or species. Dawkins argued that it is essentially a competition between replicating genes to occupy positions on chromosomes. When their phenotypic effects enhance an individual's chances of survival and reproductive success, they will tend to be passed on. Individual organisms are therefore to be thought of as vehicles by means of which genes propagate themselves. Dawkins had no problem with the obvious fact that selection operates on phenotypic effects rather than on genes. He was able to account for altruism between related individuals, where it is undeniably stronger, as producing a net benefit for the genes they share.

There nevertheless appear to be many cases of altruism between non-related individuals, especially on the part of humans. Darwin, who of course knew nothing of genetics, was puzzled by self-sacrifice and opined that groups whose members were willing to subordinate self-interest were likely to be successful in competition with less cohesive groups. This view can be adapted to yield the hypothesis that members of cohesive and therefore successful groups will be more likely to perpetuate those genes responsible for making them willing to subordinate self-interest. A group-selectionist school (Sober & Wilson, 1998) has emerged to challenge gene-selectionism along such lines. (Group-selectionists are not its only challengers.) The gene-selectionist is able to reply that just as selection operates on the phenotype, so also it may operate at group level, but neither fact invalidates the proposition that genes cause what is selected for and are in this sense the unit of selection.

Someone inclined to defend the reality of altruism might be drawn to group-selectionism on the grounds that it exists to address the 'problem', but (although I am not competent to pronounce on a very complex question) I believe this would be unwarranted. After all, the group-selectionist has still to explain why individuals behave altruistically towards members of other groups without hesitation. My challenge is to the basis of both gene- and group-selectionism, namely gene causation. For reasons explored in Chapter 1, it must be treated as weak; if causal necessity is actually jettisoned, gene causation becomes irredeemably epistemological. Either way it cannot support an explanatory theory of behaviour, far less a deterministic theory. Even phenotypic characters such as hands and hearts cannot properly be said to be caused by genes. By explaining this weakness, S-theory can close an explanatory gap while offering the outline of a theoretical structure for the synthesis of environmental factors with gene expression.

A feature manifested by biological systems at multiple levels but most notably and massively in the area of gene expression is deconstraint. Without determinism guarding the door, this concept would be able to come in from the cold. Some of the behaviour of other animals, while not altruistic, is not of obvious direct relevance to their survival or reproduction and may best be described as *exuberant*. Can birdsong or homosexuality, for example, be accounted for purely in terms of advantage? Our capacity to entertain conscious reasons for action constitutes a further domain of exception. If our behaviour is not calibrated according to a calculus of advantage, the concept of altruism may itself need revision since, at least in biological discussions, it presupposes that benefit can be weighed against cost in an extensional manner frequently at odds with how we consciously frame our actions. An individual's motivational trajectory is capable of entirely subverting notions of cost and benefit defined by the theory they are intended to confirm. Deconstraint in our case allows cultural patterns to form and then be reinforced through their socially modulated representation. A reduction of these processes would inevitably entail a loss of meaning, which often has motivational significance. At the same time a person could decide to perform an unambiguously altruistic act in order to demonstrate that it is possible. Evoking perhaps a strain of native fatalism, orthodoxy decrees that a causal chain conditioned by self-interest could in principle be found behind such a step. Let it then be found. While we wait, and provided we are willing, we have the tools to deconstrain our conceptualization of our own psychology and behaviour. The task is to do them justice while theorizing them consistently with the rest of science.

In conclusion I offer what I hope may be a thought-provoking claim: if metaphysical necessity were causal, life as we know it would not be possible. It has exploited the ontological *status quo* by means of the S-axis, which is unique to it. The S-axis supports optimizing opportunism, from the conscious down to the genetic levels. Organisms depend on deconstrained opportunism for survival: they require faculties that are thoroughly adapted but allow the greatest possible scope for adjustment to circumstances. The requisite functions are ontologically anchored in heritable physical structures, which are dependent on external nutrients and stimuli to achieve their purpose. I introduced causal insufficiency as peculiarly biological. In fact it is universal but is only exploited by forms of life. One could easily imagine an organism whose functions were causally determined: it would behave mechanically, responding predictably to stimuli, devoid of meaning and its own agenda. But the very existence of an evolved organism, with a genotype and phenotype, is predicated on the absence of causal necessity. The mechanical organism with its mechanical brain is a contradiction.

RECOMMENDED READING

If this book has stimulated an interest in philosophy (partly, after all, my intention) and you would like to take it further, I'll try to help but it is not straightforward. Bear in mind that what I have been doing is not philosophy as normally understood but a strange mutation involving evolutionary theory. Studying philosophy means learning to think philosophically, something no one has ever managed simply by reading. It requires interaction with a teacher who can force one to expose one's thought processes to scrutiny and then enable self-scrutiny. My best advice is therefore to find a class. A good teacher would also guide your reading, the risk being that a random choice of material might be incomprehensible and lead you to lose interest before you had started.

On this proviso, here are a few recommendations. If you have digested this book, none of them should be unduly taxing.

Having crossed over from the academic domain, the topic of consciousness is remarkably well served. The best single volume may now be Max Velmans's and Susan Schneider's *The Blackwell Companion to Consciousness*. The editors, a psychologist and a philosopher, have created an interdisciplinary milestone, with contributions of varying difficulty from many of the leading practitioners, presented with the non-specialist in mind. Some of the book's contributors turn up in Susan Blackmore's *Conversations on Consciousness*. She had the brilliant idea of waylaying twenty luminaries at the key conference, allowing exchanges to develop freely from the same few questions, including one about free will, and faithfully reproducing the results. Colin McGinn's *The Mysterious Flame: Conscious minds in a material world* is an accessible treatment by a leading philosopher.

More conventional introductions to philosophy fall into two categories: histories and topic-based primers. The former includes Anthony Kenny's *Brief History of Western Philosophy* and Roger Scruton's *Short History of Modern Philosophy*, the latter Thomas Nagel's *What Does It All Mean?* and Simon Blackburn's *Think*. Particularly enjoyable is Avrum Stroll's *Twentieth-Century Analytic Philosophy*, which surveys the field while making the intrinsically difficult arguments as digestible as possible and the debates as lively. Stroll also presents a considered case for the pre-eminence of Wittgenstein. A curious reader would naturally be impatient to discover what all the fuss is about and turn to him. I would strongly recommend deferring this heady gratification in favour of a searching, philosophically acute biography, Ray Monk's *Ludwig Wittgenstein*. Jonathan Barnes's *Aristotle: A very short introduction* could be an entry-point to Greek philosophy.

I have leant heavily on biological thought and as a non-biologist am indebted to two books. Ernst Mayr's beautifully written *This is Biology* is the best general introduction (and is not a textbook), while Walter Freeman's engaging *How Brains Make Up Their Minds* appears to pull the plug scientifically on computational neurology. Marc Kirschner's and John Gerhart's *The Plausibility of Life* is an eye-opening dispatch from the cutting edge of evo-devo biology. Two approaches to evolutionary theory are contrasted by Kim Sterelny in *Dawkins vs. Gould*. If your preference is for intellectual history, do not be put off by the title of Thomas Kuhn's luminous *The Structure of Scientific Revolutions*. His duel with Karl Popper is set in deep context by Steve Fuller in *Kuhn vs. Popper*. Kenan Malik's *Man, Beast and Zombie: What science can and cannot tell us about human nature* is a wide-ranging investigation by a neurobiologist who is also a historian of ideas.

REFERENCES & BIBLIOGRAPHY

Abzhanov, A., Protas, M., Grant, B., Grant, P. and Tabin, C. 2004. Bmp4 and morphological variation of beaks in Darwin's finches. *Science* 305: 1462.

Anscombe, G. 2000 (1957). *Intention*. Cambridge, MA: Harvard University Press.

―――― 1971. *Causality and Determinism*. Cambridge: Cambridge University Press. Extract (Causality and Determination) in Sosa and Tooley, 1993.

Austin, J. 1962. *How to Do Things with Words*. Oxford: Oxford University Press.

Bach, K. 2007. Regressions in pragmatics (and semantics). In N. Burton-Roberts (ed.), *Pragmatics (Palgrave Advances)*. Basingstoke: Palgrave Macmillan.

Chalmers, D. 1996. *The Conscious Mind*. New York: Oxford University Press.

Davidson, D. 1963. Actions, reasons and causes. *Journal of Philosophy* 60. Also in Mele, 1997.

Dawkins, R. 1976 (2006 3rd edn.). *The Selfish Gene*. Oxford: Oxford University Press.

―――― 1982 (1999 2nd edn.). *The Extended Phenotype*. Oxford: Oxford University Press.

Dedrick, D. 1996. Can color be reduced to anything? *Philosophy of Science*, Supplement to Issue 63.

Dretske, F. 1995. *Naturalizing the Mind*. Cambridge, MA: MIT Press.

Dummett, M. 2006. *Thought and Reality*. Oxford: Clarendon Press.

Fodor, J. 2000. *The Mind Doesn't Work That Way*. Cambridge, MA: MIT Press.

Foster, J. 2000. *The Nature of Perception*. Oxford: Clarendon Press.

Frankfurt, H. 1978. The problem of action. *American Philosophical Quarterly* 15: 157-162. Also in Mele, 1997.

Freeman, W. 2001. *How Brains Make Up Their Minds*. New York: Columbia University Press.

Frege, G. 1892. Über Sinn und Bedeutung. *Zeitschrift für Philosophie und philosophische Kritik*, NF 100: 25-50. Also in Moore, 1993 (as *On sense and reference*).

Gettier, E. 1963. Is justified true belief knowledge? *Analysis* 23: 121-123.

Grice, H. 1975. Logic and conversation. In P. Cole and J. Morgan (eds.), *Syntax and Semantics 3: Pragmatics*. New York: Academic Press.

Hacker, P. 1996. *Wittgenstein's Place in Twentieth-Century Analytic Philosophy*. Oxford: Blackwell.

Hockney, D. 2001. *Secret Knowledge*. London: Thames and Hudson.

Hume, D. 2000 (1739-1740). *A Treatise of Human Nature*. Oxford: Oxford University Press.

―――― 1999 (1748). *An Enquiry Concerning Human Understanding*. Oxford: Oxford University Press.

REFERENCES & BIBLIOGRAPHY

Jablonka, E. and Lamb, M. 1995. *Epigenetic Inheritance and Evolution*. Oxford: Oxford University Press.

Johnsson, J. and Åkerman, A. 1998. Watch and learn: preview of the fighting ability of opponents alters contest behaviour in rainbow trout. *Animal Behaviour* 56: 771-776.

Kim, J. 2005. *Physicalism, or Something Near Enough*. Princeton: Princeton University Press.

Kirschner, M. and Gerhart, J. 2005. *The Plausibility of Life*. New Haven: Yale University Press.

Kripke, S. 1972. *Naming and Necessity*. Cambridge, MA: Harvard University Press.

Kuhn, T. 1962 (1996 3rd edn.). *The Structure of Scientific Revolutions*. Chicago: University of Chicago Press.

―――― 1990. Dubbing and redubbing: the vulnerability of rigid designation. In C. Wade Savage (ed.), *Scientific Theories*. Minneapolis: University of Minnesota Press.

Lehar, S. 2003. Gestalt isomorphism and the primacy of subjective conscious experience. *Behavioral and Brain Sciences* 26 (4).

Lewis, D. 1973. Causation. *Journal of Philosophy* 70: 556-567. Also in Sosa and Tooley, 1993.

Li, W., Feng, Z., Sternberg, P. and Xu, X. 2006. A *C. elegans* stretch receptor neuron revealed by a mechanosensitive TRP channel homologue. *Nature* 440: 684-687.

Libet, B. 1981. The experimental evidence for subjective referral of a sensory experience backwards in time. *Philosophy of Science* 48: 181-197.

Libet, B., Gleason, C., Wright, E. and Pearl, D. 1983. Time of conscious intention to act in relation to onset of cerebral activity (readiness-potential). The unconscious initiation of a freely voluntary act. *Brain* 106: 623-642.

Lighthill, J. 1973. Artificial Intelligence: a general survey. In *Artificial Intelligence: A paper symposium*, Science Research Council.

Locke, J. 2008 (1689). *An Essay Concerning Human Understanding*. Oxford: Oxford University Press.

Lyons, W. 1995. *Approaches to Intentionality*. Oxford: Clarendon Press.

MacLean, P. 1973. *A Triune Concept of the Brain and Behaviour*. Toronto: University of Toronto Press.

Mameli, M. 2004. Nongenetic selection and nongenetic inheritance. *British Journal for the Philosophy of Science* 55: 35-71.

McGinn, C. 2004. *Consciousness and its Objects*. Oxford: Clarendon Press.

Mele, A. (ed.) 1997. *The Philosophy of Action*. Oxford: Oxford University Press.

Mill, J. 2002 (1843). *A System of Logic*. Honolulu: University Press of the Pacific.

Milner, A. and Goodale, M. 1995. *The Visual Brain in Action*. Oxford: Oxford University Press.

Mitchell, T., Shinkareva, S., Carlson, A., Chang, K., Malave, V., Mason, R. and Just, M. 2008. Predicting human brain activity associated with the meanings of nouns. *Science* 320: 1191-1195.

Moore, A. (ed.) 1993. *Meaning and Reference*. Oxford: Oxford University Press.

Nagel, T. 1986. *The View from Nowhere*. New York: Oxford University Press.

Noë, A. 2005. *Action in Perception*. Cambridge, MA: MIT Press.

Noë, A. and Thompson, E. (eds.) 2002. *Vision and Mind*. Cambridge, MA: MIT Press.

O'Regan, J. and Noë, A. 2001. A sensorimotor account of vision and visual consciousness. *Behavioral and Brain Sciences* 24 (5): 883-917.

Praetorius, N. 2007. The problems of consciousness and content in theories of perception. *Phenomenology and the Cognitive Sciences* 6: 349–367.

Price, H. and Corry, R. (eds.) 2007. *Causation, Physics and the Constitution of Reality*. Oxford: Clarendon Press.

Putnam, H. 1973. Meaning and reference. *Journal of Philosophy* 70 (19): 699-711. Also in Moore, 1993.

―――― 1975. The meaning of 'meaning'. In *Mind, Language and Reality: Philosophical Papers Volume 2*. Cambridge: Cambridge University Press.

Quine, W. 1970 (1986 2nd edn.). *Philosophy of Logic*. Cambridge, MA: Harvard University Press.

Revonsuo, A. 2006. *Inner Presence*: *Consciousness as a biological phenomenon*. Cambridge, MA: MIT Press.

Russell, B. 1913. On the notion of cause. *Proceedings of the Aristotelian Society* 13: 1-26. In *Mysticism and Logic and Other Essays*. London: Routledge.

Schaffer, J. 2007. The metaphysics of causation. *The Stanford Encyclopedia of Philosophy*, E. N. Zalta (ed.), URL = <http://plato.stanford.edu/archives/fall2008/entries/causation-metaphysics/>

Searle, J. 1969. *Speech Acts*. Cambridge: Cambridge University Press.

―――― 1980. Minds, brains and programs. *Behavioral and Brain Sciences* 3: 417-424.

―――― 1983. *Intentionality*. Cambridge: Cambridge University Press.

―――― 1995. *The Construction of Social Reality*. London: Allen Lane.

Slobodchikoff, C., Perla, B. and Verdolin, J. 2009. *Prairie Dogs: Communication and community in an animal society*. Cambridge, MA: Harvard University Press.

Smith, A. 2002. *The Problem of Perception*. Cambridge, MA: Harvard University Press.

Sober, E. and Wilson, D. 1998. *Unto Others: The evolution and psychology of unselfish behavior*. Cambridge, MA: Harvard University Press.

Sosa, E. and Tooley, M. (eds.) 1993. *Causation*. Oxford: Oxford University Press.

Strawson, P. 1950. On referring. *Mind* 59: 320-344. Also in Moore, 1993.

Velmans, M. 2000. *Understanding Consciousness*. London: Routledge.

Watson, G. (ed.) 2003 (2nd edn.). *Free Will*. Oxford: Oxford University Press.

Wittgenstein, L. 2001 (1922). *Tractatus Logico-Philosophicus*. London: Routledge.

―――― 2001 (1953). *Philosophical Investigations*. Oxford: Blackwell.

Wright, J. (1983). *The Sceptical Realism of David Hume*. Manchester: Manchester University Press.

INDEX

a priori/a posteriori judgments 80, 89-90, 93, 135-137, 146
Abzhanov, A. 33
afferent 11, 15, 17, 28, 36, 49, 70, 130
   brain's afferent condition of satisfaction 28, 50, 130
   neurological novelty 36
   neurology of parsing 70
Åkerman, A. 15
Anscombe, G. 119-120, 146
   on causal necessity 146
   on intention 119-120
Anstoss 45-47
appetitive desire 104-105, 116, 150
Aristarchus 132
Aristotle 1, 68, 86, 146
artificial intelligence 3-4, 21, 52, 70-71
assigned function 56-57, 60, 70, 126, 129, 131
Austin, J. 94

Bach, K. 91
behaviourism 22
binding process 20, 27, 30, 40, 61, 100
Blackmore, S. 149
Bruner, J. 133

C. elegans 14-16
causation 7-8, 23-24, 26, 49, 136-146
   by conscious states 8, 49, 106
   by genes 152-153
   causal insufficiency 23, 31, 147
   causal necessity 136-139, 144-146
   causal theory of action 115
   causal theory of perception 26
   causal theory of reference 69
   constitutive 7-8, 23-24, 144, 145, 147
   elimination of 140-141
   in the law 143
   linear 7-8, 12, 42, 147
   metaphysical concept 26
   scientific vs. supernatural 138
Chalmers, D. 10
   hard problem of consciousness 10-11, 15, 23, 31
chaos 12, 27, 36, 42, 141, 145
   teleological chaos 36
circularity 26-27, 42, 51, 69, 78
cognitive dissonance 99
cognitivism 4-5, 9, 10, 21, 30, 92, 106
collegium 125-126
colour vision 5, 44-45
combinatorial explosion 4, 36
compatibilism, 149
computation 2-5, 12, 14, 21-22, 30, 53, 70, 106
condition of satisfaction 25-26
connotation 64-65
consciousness 4-5, 8, 13-15, 18-20, 28, 30-31, 37-38, 43, 49-50
   and cognitivism 4-5
   as condition of satisfaction 28
   as evolutionary fact 20, 49-50
   attribution to other animals 14-15, 49-50
   conscious reasons 116-118, 150-151
   constitutive mechanisms 43
   control of motor behaviour 18, 112
   ephemerality of conscious states 30-31
   hard problem 10, 15, 31
   machine consciousness 5, 37-38
   neural correlates of 30-31, 43, 51
   necessitation by conscious states 30-31

perceptual construal 40-42, 134
  by other animals 41
  phenomenal vs. reflective 13-14
  ventral & dorsal streams 19
contingent 62, 70, 80, 86-88
correlation 10, 23, 30, 42, 52
brain/mental states 30-31, 43, 51
genotype/phenotype 23
Cyc project 3, 78

Darwinism 138, 153
Davidson, D. 115-116
Dawkins, R. 54, 152
  The Extended Phenotype 54
  gene-selectionism 152
deconstraint 32-33, 154
Democritus of Abdera 1, 86, 132
Dennett, D. 21
Descartes, R. 10
  Cartesian framework 10, 20, 53, 131
Dretske, F. 38-42
dualism 9-10
Dummett, M. 78

efferent 11, 16-17, 36, 71-72, 112
  brain's efferent condition of satisfaction 28
  efference in perception 17
  language use as behaviour 71-72
  neurological novelty 36
Einstein, A. 134, 140-141
emergence 8-9, 144-145
  higher-level properties 144-145
ephemerality
  of conscious states 31
  of phenotypic extension 57
epigenetic inheritance 34-36
epistemology 6-7, 22, 29, 80, 129-131
  causation epistemological 145
  epistemological meaning 22, 29
  epistemological phenomena 6-7
  epistemological S-axis 56, 129-131
  laws of nature 145-146
  perception as epistemological 50-51

evo-devo biology 32
externalism 42, 51, 67, 70
  natural kind externalism 67

Frege, G. 64-65, 82
Freeman, W. 12, 51

gene expression 28, 32, 34-36, 43, 154
genotype 23-24, 27-29, 31, 35-36, 130, 155
Gerhart, J. 32-33
gestalt 63
Gettier, E. 84
Goodale, M. 19
Grice, P. 91-94

Hockney, D. 100
Hoffman, L. 143
homunculus fallacy 38
Hume, D. 12-13, 26, 137-139, 141, 144, 149
  on causation 137-139, 141
  Touchstone 12-13, 16

idealism 5, 48, 82
  anti-realism 53, 82
identity statement 80, 86, 88
incorporand 27, 28, 40, 42, 59, 130
inference 40
intension 64, 72, 77, 79-83, 88, 110-114, 134
  distinguished from sense 72
  intensional verbs 79-83, 110-114, 120
intentionality 25-26, 38, 40, 43, 123
  of intention 123
  of mental states 25-26
  of objects 38
internalism 42, 51, 53, 131
  evolutionary internalism 131

Jablonka, E. 34
Johnson, S. 149
Johnsson, J. 15
Just, M. 71

INDEX

Kirschner, M. 32-33
knowledge 62, 84-86, 131
   repository 62, 75, 85, 119, 125
Kripke, S. 68-69, 78-80, 87-88,
   133-134
   essentialism (vs. Kuhn) 133-134
   modality/possible worlds 87-88
   necessary *a posteriori* 80
   rigid designation 68-69, 78-80
Kuhn, T. 131-135
   Kuhnian paradigm 131-134, 141

Lamb, M. 34
laws of nature 7, 135-136, 145-146,
   148
Lehar, S. 37-38
Lenat, D. 3
Libet, B. 17-18, 151
Lighthill, J. 4
Locke, J. 44, 46-47

MacLean, P. 16
Mameli, M. 35
meaning 21-23, 27, 29-30, 54-55,
   60-61
   and reference 65-66, 69
   artistic 98
   expressed vs. realized 29, 55,
      60, 62
   meant behaviour 112-114
   of satisfaciend 27, 54-55
   of signal 61
   perceptual 39-40
   synonymous with intending
      107-109
   word meaning 63-64
metaphysics, 25-26, 53, 80, 87,
   144-149
   of biological function 53
   of S-axis 49, 53
   necessity 139, 144-149, 155
   possible worlds 87
   proposition as metaphysical 76
Mill, J. 64, 68
Milner, D. 19
Minsky, M. 71
Molyneaux's Question 46
Moore, G. 83

motivational trajectory 117, 129,
   152, 154

name/naming 61, 64, 67-70, 102-3
natural kinds 67-69, 71
naturalization 5, 67, 70
Newton, I. 20, 81, 132
   laws 135-136, 140
Noë, A. 17, 18
normativity 55, 72-73, 75, 125,
   150-151
   epistemic 75
   influences on behaviour 150-151
   of word use 72-73

ontology 5-6, 8, 23, 26, 29, 48,
   129-131, 135, 144
   of organisms 48, 144
   of subjectivity 29
   of the S-axis 129-131, 145, 155
   ontological constraint 146
optical illusion 19, 22
O'Regan, K. 18

parsing 19-20, 21, 40-42, 58-59,
   61, 69, 70-71, 100, 134
   relation to naming 69-70
percept 20, 27, 48, 51, 124
   as satisfaciend 61, 124, 130
pet fish experiment, 63
phenotype, 23-25, 30-36
phenotypic extension, 54-60, 130,
   148
   male/female, 57-58
physicalism, 9-10, 31
plasticity, 31-36, 40, 42, 63
Popper, K. 53, 133
Postman, L. 133
Praetorius, N. 26
prediction 110, 119-120
promising 94-98
proprioception 15, 17, 45-48
Putnam, H. 67, 80-81, 133-134
   essentialism (vs. Kuhn) 133-134
   natural kind externalism 67
   Twin Earth experiment 80-81
Pythagoras 101

Quine, W. 77

realism 5-7, 48, 99-100
   Hume's 138
referent 65-66
representationalism 37-42
Revonsuo, A. 13, 43
Russell, B. 68, 140-141, 145
   definite description 68
   on causation 140-141, 145

S-axis 26-27, 29, 48, 61, 109, 113, 116, 129-131, 145, 147-148
   real/epistemological 129-131
satisfaciend, 25-30, 36, 42, 54-56, 61, 93, 104-105, 109, 117, 118, 124, 125, 126, 128, 130, 148-149
   expressed meaning of 29
   internal to organism 61, 124, 130-131
   organism not a 126, 151
   phenotypic extension as 54-56
   sentence as 61-64, 84, 93
Schaffer, J. 141
Searle, J. 21-22, 25-26, 94
   Chinese Room 21-22, 70
   intentionality 25-26
   promising 94-96
sentence 61-64, 92
   as statement 62, 66, 74-77, 92-94
   contingent 62, 80, 86
   sense of 62-63
sentience 13-16, 20, 42, 49-50
signalling 57-58, 61, 64, 66, 102-103
speech act 94-95
   as action 113
Slobodchikoff, C. 102-103
Smith, A. 45
Sober, E. 153
Sraffa. P. 82
symbol-grounding problem 70

teleology 27, 54
   teleological chaos 36
   teleological reason 115-118

truth 66, 75-78, 86-90, 129
   truth conditions 75-78, 92
Turing, A. 2, 21-22
   Turing machine 2

units of selection 152-153
uranium-238 146-147

Xu, S. 15

vervet monkey 57, 103
voluntary action 114, 120

Wilson, D. 153
Wittgenstein 22, 73-74, 81-82, 93, 94, 119, 127-129, 133
   games and institutions 127-129
   logical form of propositions 81-82
   Philosophical Investigations 22, 82
   private language 73-74
   rule-following 22
   Tractatus Logico-Philosophicus 82
Wright, J. 138